Designing with Succulents

Designing with Succulents

Debra Lee Baldwin

Timber Press
Portland, Oregon

Page 2: The color, shape, and form of a dragon tree's foliage repeat those of a nearby dasylirion in Jeanne Meadow's Fallbrook, California, succulent garden.

Opposite: *Agave* 'Sharkskin'

First edition published 2007.

Photography, design, and location credits appear on page 292.

Published in 2017 by Timber Press, Inc.

The Haseltine Building
133 S.W. Second Avenue, Suite 450
Portland, Oregon 97204-3527

timberpress.com

Printed in China

Text design by Laken Wright
Cover design by Hillary Caudle

Library of Congress Cataloging-in-Publication Data

Names: Baldwin, Debra Lee, author.
Title: Designing with succulents: create a lush garden of waterwise plants / Debra Lee Baldwin.
Description: Second edition. | Portland, Oregon: Timber Press, 2017. | First edition published 2007. | Includes bibliographical references and index.
Identifiers: LCCN 2016045511 | ISBN 9781604697087 (hardcover)
Subjects: LCSH: Succulent plants. | Gardens—Design. | Gardening.
Classification: LCC SB438 .B25 2017 | DDC 635.9/525—dc23 LC record available at https://lccn.loc.gov/2016045511ISBN-13: 978-1-60469-708-7

A catalog record for this book is also available from the British Library.

To Jeff, Art, and Sandra

Contents

Succulent Landscape Essentials: Plan and Design Your Dream Garden

Orchestrating the Ideal Site for Succulents • Six Design Must-Dos for a Great-Looking Garden • Enhancing Your Succulent Showplace • Transforming Your Front Yard with Succulents • Terraces That Turn Hillsides into Gardens • Your Garden, from Dream to Reality

Specialty Gardens That Showcase Succulents

Boulder and Rock Gardens • Seaside and Sea-Theme Gardens • Desert Gardens with Style • Firewise Gardens • Succulents in the Sky: Green Roof Gardens • Cold-Clmate Succulent Gardens • Creative Container Gardens • Geometric and Tapestry Gardens • Diminutive Landscapes

Success Secrets for Succulents

Planting Tips and Techniques • Water and Fertilizer • Grooming Your Succulents • Pest and Damage Control • Weed Control • Cultivating Succulents in Challenging Climates • Propagation: New Plants from Old • Care and Feeding of Container Succulents

Preface

A Decade of Innovation in Succulent Design

The world of succulent design has advanced so significantly since the first edition of *Designing with Succulents* was released in 2007 that this second edition is a complete rewrite—in effect, a new book. It showcases the cleverness and creativity of numerous designers and gardening enthusiasts, many of whom used the first edition as a starting point.

When I was writing the first edition, many varieties we now take for granted, such as echeverias, were nearly unknown. The gardening public thought of succulents as cactus or jade and dismissed the entire category as too spiny or common. If finding enough sophisticated, well-designed in-ground gardens to fill a book was challenging, identifying the plants proved even more so. Horticulturists, growers, and collectors—by and large pleasant eccentrics who didn't do email—would agree on genera but not necessarily species or cultivars.

Since then, interest in water-storing plants has surged due to the West's ongoing drought and wildfire concerns. Moreover, the gardening public, grown weary of trying to replicate English flower gardens, has become interested in form and foliage. Time-stressed homeowners want plants that won't die if neglected and that look the same for months. Women, who now constitute the majority of succulent aficionados, have become captivated by rosette varieties. Brides and florists have discovered that pale blue, dove gray, and teal echeverias lend a fresh look to bouquets and centerpieces. Numerous succulent-oriented businesses have sprung up as growers, hybridizers, designers, and nursery owners have scrambled to meet the demand.

The popularity of succulents is also evidenced by their strong Internet presence, frequent social media mentions, and use as decor in movies, television shows, and advertisements. It's much easier to identify succulents nowadays, thanks to a greater number of experts, enthusiasts, and collectors, many of them devoted to certain genera (such as *Aloe* or *Haworthia*) or subcategories (such as caudiciforms or cacti).

When I began working on this celebratory tenth anniversary edition, my biggest challenge was the opposite of what I faced with the first edition: an overabundance of beautifully designed succulent gardens. Much time went into selecting best-of-the-best photos to illustrate design ideas and to showcase this new edition's featured gardens.

Because I enjoy cultivating a wide variety of succulents as well as using them to create a visual adventure, my own half acre is a living laboratory of plants plus ideas gleaned from designers, fellow gardeners, and trial and error. Photos of my garden appear in the introduction and elsewhere, especially the chapter on specialty gardens.

You, too, can create the low-water garden of your dreams. Whether you're a longtime fan of fleshy leaved plants or new to them, it's my pleasure to share with you, in these proudly updated pages, the beauty, practicality, and creativity inherent in designing with succulents.

OPPOSITE, LEFT Homeowner Elisabeth Matthys, shown here, asked designer Linda Bresler to create a landscape similar to the one pictured on the cover of the first edition of *Designing with Succulents*. The outcome received *San Diego Home/ Garden* magazine's prestigious Garden of the Year award.

OPPOSITE, RIGHT After it opened in 2011, the Succulent Café in Oceanside, California, became a destination for enthusiasts worldwide. Noreen Fenton of Succulent Surroundings came to visit from Santa Rosa, nearly 500 miles away.

Echeverias pair well with roses in bridal bouquets and can later be planted as a living memento of the event.

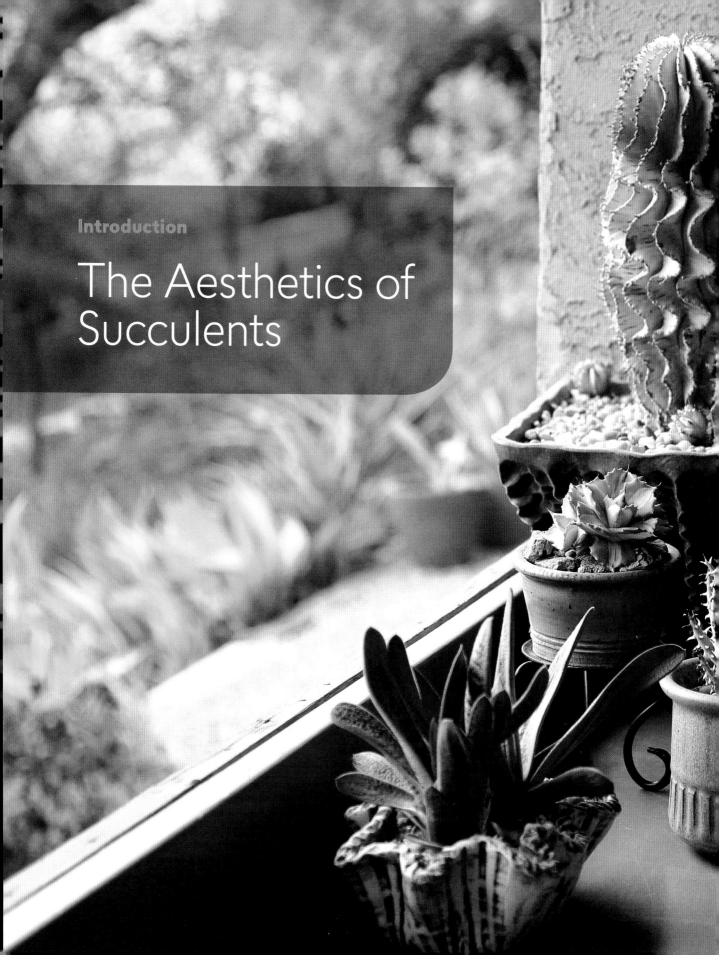

The Aesthetics of Succulents

Succulent describes any plant that survives drought by storing water in its leaves, stems, or roots. These plants were far from my mind when I began gardening in my early thirties. Because I wanted big, bold, beautiful flowers, I planted cannas and rose bushes, despite the fact that in southern California (USDA zone 9) rain falls minimally and mostly in February, the soil lacks nutrients, and inland temperatures range from 25 to 105°F. From spring through fall, such plants continually need mulching, fertilizing, pruning, spraying, irrigating, and deadheading.

As a garden photojournalist, I was influenced by editors, design professionals, colleagues, homeowners, and horticulturists who believed that gardening is an endeavor that ought to suit the region. It was my job to communicate via words and photos why certain residential outdoor environments were innovative and appealing—not only visually but also practically. As I strove to entertain and enlighten the gardening public, I became inspired myself.

One midwinter, when my garden consisted of pruned and naked rose bushes, cannas with frost-burned leaves, and perennials that had been cut to the ground, I visited the garden of horticulturist Patrick Anderson midway between Los Angeles and San Diego. Despite its poor soil and lack of irrigation, his garden was lush and colorful. It was the first time I had seen large aloes in a garden setting. The ensuing article reflected my fascination: "Fleshy green monsters in Patrick Anderson's Fallbrook garden look like they might snap him up if he turns his back," it began. "They're giant succulents, and Anderson's half-acre hillside showcases hundreds of unusual ones." I described aloes that "pierce the sky like exotic torchbearers, hot orange against cool blue," and agaves that "sprawl like squids, or explode upward like fistfuls of knives."

I noticed how two or three varieties of succulents selected for shape, color, and texture create elegant and eye-catching vignettes. Succulents with curved or undulating leaves suggest motion, which makes any garden more interesting. Moreover, like seashells and snowflakes, succulent foliage forms patterns that illustrate nature's innate geometry and that are mesmerizing when repeated.

I soon learned firsthand that in a warm, dry climate, succulents and similarly low-water perennials make sense economically, aesthetically, and ecologically. *Aeonium arboreum* and *A. haworthii*, *Agave americana* 'Marginata', and *Bulbine frutescens* proved trouble-free— as did the aloes, sedums, senecios, kalanchoes, and

RIGHT It was in Patrick Anderson's garden in Fallbrook, California, that I had my succulent epiphany. In the foreground are *Agave guiengola* and *Aloe* ×'David Verity'.

BOTTOM Wholesale growers start succulents in flats, then ship them to nurseries across the country. Those shown here are mostly cold-hardy sedums and ice plants.

graptopetalums that followed. I found succulents easy to propagate and appealing wherever I put them.

I began hunting gardens that showcased succulents and over the years have discovered them throughout the West and as far away as Hawaii, Texas, Florida, Pennsylvania, and New England. This book, the result, offers numerous alternatives to traditional lawn-and-flowerbed landscapes, shows what's possible when succulents shine as primary garden elements, and explains how to cultivate these versatile plants in the ground and in containers.

It's an exciting time to be a succulent aficionado; numerous ornamental hybrids have recently been released or are in production. In years to come, watch for named cultivars with greater heat and cold tolerance, longer bloom cycles, multicolored flowers, disease resistance, and leaves that are vividly hued, variegated, or textured.

Succulent gardens far and wide

Succulents range from tall trees to ground covers with rice-size leaves. Among their native habitats are South American jungles, California's coastal cliffs, high-elevation mountains in Africa, and arid Arizona plains. In cultivation, they look good alongside meandering pathways, in formal settings with geometric lines, in rock gardens, and in pots on patios, balconies, and rooftops—to name a few of many possible settings.

Most, but not all, of the succulents included here come from areas of the world that are hot and dry and that receive minimal rainfall. These plants are best suited to USDA zones 9 and 10, although they can survive outdoors in zones 8 and 11 with adequate protection from frost, excessive heat, and moisture. This ideal climate is found sporadically in latitudes from 20 to 40 degrees, especially in marine-influenced, nontropical areas of the U.S. South and Southwest, Mexico, Pakistan, northern India, eastern China, Taiwan, southern Japan, South America, South Africa, Australia, New Zealand, and the Mediterranean.

Can you grow succulents?

It's possible for anyone, anywhere, to cultivate any kind of succulent. The plants like the same conditions you do: warmth, fresh air, sunlight, and dryness. Moreover, what once was exotic is now available at your local nursery or via mail order. Even potentially immense succulents stay small and manageable in pots, which are portable and can be moved and sheltered when the weather turns too hot, too cold, or too wet for their liking.

Those succulents native to warm, arid climates (the majority) are generally frost tender and don't thrive in cold soils that retain moisture for weeks on end. Consequently, the farther north or higher in elevation you go from the ideal climate for succulents (which in the United States is southern California and along the West Coast from the Bay Area south), the fewer varieties you can easily grow in the ground year-round. If you live in, say, Iowa or Oregon, pay particular attention to the section on cold-climate succulents in the chapter on specialty gardens.

As with any plants, the more you know about and strive to replicate (within reason) their native habitats, the greater your likelihood of success. You'll find general information about succulent care and cultivation in this book, and info specific to each plant in an alphabetical directory of varieties. If this sounds daunting, keep in mind that succulents are the closest thing to plastic in the plant kingdom. Flora that originates in some of the earth's most challenging climates will likely survive under your care.

Sempervivums (hens and chicks) proliferate in a Washington garden along with hardy cholla and paddle cacti.

My own garden's makeover

Ironically, authoring several books about succulents nearly caused me to stop gardening. Writing, lecturing, and traveling left little time for it. Once lush with fruit trees and flowers, the rocky half acre in the foothills north of San Diego where my husband and I had lived for a quarter century was shabby and overgrown. The succulents I'd planted over the years needed rescuing from aggressive perennials like Mexican evening primrose, centranthus, and matilija poppies. The few roses that had survived looked spindly and odd alongside large agaves.

Revamping the garden was much like creating this second edition of *Designing with Succulents*: a giant editing job. A lot needed to go and a comparable amount to be added. A big project, but what's the point of having a passion if you don't pursue it? Of acquiring knowledge if you don't apply it? I wanted the garden to reflect what I'd learned about design as well as succulents. It helped, too, that I know every square inch of the land—its orientation to the sun throughout the seasons, which areas are vulnerable to cold or scorching heat, what the soil lacks or is blessed with, and how the slope (which is steep in places) erodes during storms.

Despite my renewed enthusiasm, there was no denying I'd slowed a bit. Often I was dismayed to discover I'd spent hours (hours!) caught up in perfecting a few square feet. But after a fed-up inner voice said, "How can someone be wasting her time if she enjoys what she's doing?" I allowed myself goal-free gazing. Birds emerged. Lizards did push-ups. And as always, surrounding hills became gold tipped too soon.

Creating a garden is one of life's great pleasures, not to be rushed or denied. What does it matter if visitors come and it isn't finished? Unlike a book, a garden never is.

Succulents in artist-
designed pots bask in bright
but not intense light on
an outdoor countertop.
A photo of the garden on
stretched canvas blends
this transition area with the
garden beyond.

Prickly pear cactus thrives in nutrient-
poor, rocky soil and gets by on rainfall.
To make the plants more interesting, I
grasped their pads with tongs and used
a knife to carve dancing ladies. Their
"bonfire" is a grasslike bromeliad.

Near the desert section's dry creek bed, a barrel cactus cat appears startled by a horned lizard (a lucky find at a thrift store).

One goal of my garden's redo was to use large agaves (such as this variegated *Agave americana*) as focal points. In the foreground is a jewel box garden by San Diego designer Laura Eubanks.

Above my garden's "dry lily pond" is an overturned urn spilling *Othonna capensis*. Horizontal opuntia paddles suggest lily pads; graptoveria rosettes, water lilies. The topdressing is pumice, tumbled glass, and flat floral marbles.

Acacia trees and native oaks provide succulents with shade in summer and frost protection in winter. The notch in the retaining wall is a built-in bench overlooking the garden below.

The succulents and cacti mentioned in this book are by no means all that exist or that are available but rather those best suited to residential gardens. It's a blessing of the twenty-first century—and one we take for granted—that we can possess such plants. Kalanchoes from Madagascar, for example, were unknown in the United States in 1950. And some of the toughest and showiest of succulents are hybrids introduced recently.

Your guide to succulent design, care, and selection

This book's initial chapter provides suggestions for planning and preparing your garden, including tips on soil amendment and irrigation. You'll discover the basic principles of landscape design—scale and proportion, repetition, contrast, emphasis, shape and texture, and color—and learn how to apply these to create your own succulent showplace. As you conceptualize your ideal landscape, you'll also want to consider various enhancements, such as water features, dry streambeds, and pathway borders. Plus, you'll discover how to transform your front yard into a welcoming, low-maintenance entry garden, and you'll view options for streetside areas and slopes.

The second chapter suggests creative ideas for personalizing your garden by using succulents to meet a need or illustrate a theme. Here you'll find succulents for green roofs; desert, beach, and boulder gardens; geometric and tapestry plantings; miniature landscapes; and more.

Although few pests bother succulents, you'll learn how to control those that do in the third chapter, on plant care. You'll also find out how to grow succulents in climates different from their warm, dry native habitats, and how to propagate new plants from existing ones.

Use "Succulents A to Z" to familiarize yourself with specific varieties. Browse it to discover new ones that appeal to you and to learn more about the succulents you already have. Pay particular attention to a plant's size at maturity, which has practical as well as aesthetic implications.

To help you achieve a pleasing variety of colors, shapes, heights, and sizes, design-oriented plant lists group tall, treelike, and immense succulents; midsize and shrub varieties; small, low-growing, and ground-cover succulents; and those of various colors. The chapter on waterwise companion plants lists trees, shrubs, ground covers, bulbs, annuals, and perennials with cultivation requirements similar to those of succulents, which thus can be combined with the latter to add variety.

Directional references throughout the book (such as "north-facing" and "south side") apply to the Northern Hemisphere; readers south of the equator should adjust the information accordingly. Also, references to the Southwest refer to the southwestern United States.

Succulents can serve as a three-dimensional creative medium for landscape designers and anyone who loves to garden. Few plants are as sculptural or make such statements in the landscape. With this book as your guide, you'll transform your own garden into an open-air gallery of vibrant, living art objects, perfectly suited to your tastes, location, and lifestyle.

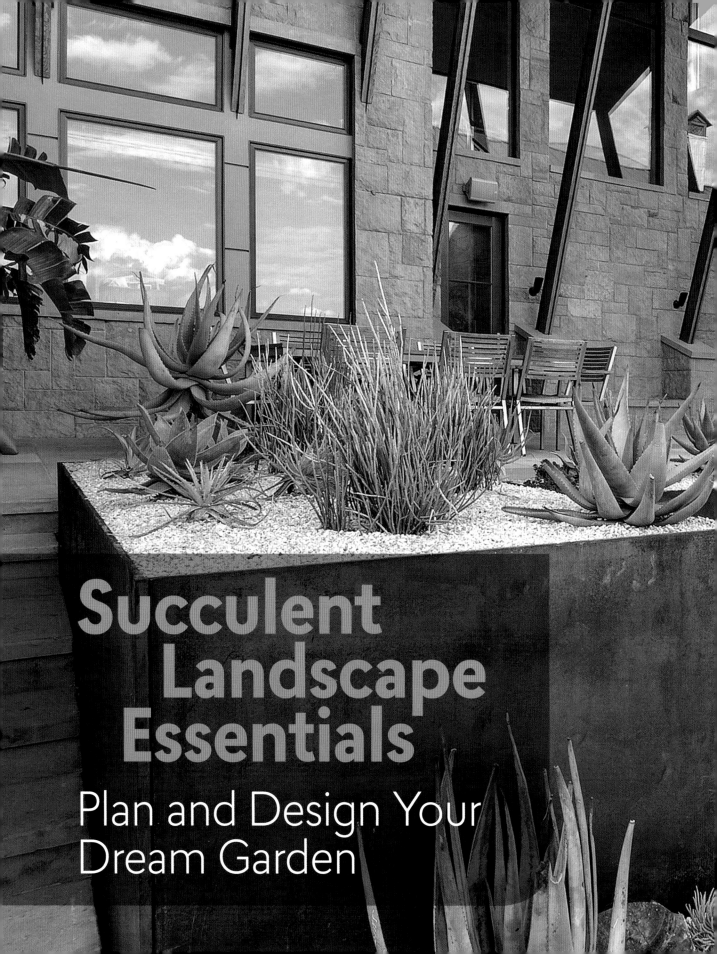

Succulent Landscape Essentials

Plan and Design Your Dream Garden

My goal is to help you design a garden you love that's uniquely yours—one that meets your requirements yet also unleashes the artist within you. This chapter explains how to prepare your canvas for planting by creating an environment in which succulents and other low-water plants will thrive, and then compose a garden that perfectly expresses your personality.

Every time you add a succulent to your collection, whether in the ground or in a container, evaluate not only where it'll do well but also where it'll look good. This, at its most elemental, is garden design. On the other end of the spectrum, orchestrating a truly great garden is a type of performance art. An expert designer understands and applies essential principles of design, and keeps viewers and visitors in mind with the goal of delighting them. Once you know how the pros achieve this, you'll understand why you like certain landscapes and find others lacking, and will better envision the potential of your own.

From standard lot to succulent sanctuary

Joan Field, a longtime member of California's Central Coast Cactus and Succulent Society, and her husband, Bob, wanted an inviting, colorful garden to serve as the view from their home's bedroom and dining room windows. With the help of landscape designer Gabriel Frank of Gardens by Gabriel in Morro Bay and Nick Wilkinson of Grow nursery in Cambria, they terraced a steep slope by creating retaining walls of interlocking Europa tumbled blocks. They also replaced a backyard lawn with decomposed granite pathways plus elevated islands of succulents and low-water companion plants. These mounded areas consist of planter mix, compost, coarse sand, and perlite. Frank moved plants, still in their nursery pots, around the site "until they looked just right," Bob recalls.

The maritime climate of the location (Pismo Beach, California) is frost free, and the south-facing garden basks in all-day sun. A drip system runs once every three weeks. Frank notes that many of the perennials that made the garden lush at first, such as penstemon and gaillardia, waned after a few years, leaving succulents to "form the bones of the garden." These include *Dasylirion wheeleri*, *Agave desmetiana*, *Euphorbia ingens*, *E. ammak*, and aloes. Among the companion plants that endured are *Cordyline australis*, *Ceanothus* 'Wheeler Canyon', lorapetalum, and *Grevillea* 'Austraflora Fanfare'. "There's only a handful of xeric [waterwise] plants that can keep up with the low-maintenance and low-water needs of succulents," says Frank. "This has been a great testing ground."

Midsize aloes repeat throughout the garden. Among them are *Aloe striata* (coral aloe), which blooms in the spring. Variegated *Agave desmetiana*, right, doesn't get much larger than this.

A topdressing of slate chips conceals bare spots, helps hold moisture in the soil, and visually adds a finishing touch. In addition to aloes, aeoniums, and graptoverias, *Cleistocactus strausii* (silver torch cactus) and *Leucadendron* 'Jester', a low-water shrub from Australia, provide contrasting colors, forms, and textures. Variegated *Yucca gloriosa* 'Bright Star' sparkles at lower right.

Garden beds and terraces form a backdrop for the alfresco dining area. To appear integral to the garden, the concrete curves and has a warm hue.

In the foreground are a fountainlike beschorneria, ×*Graptoveria* 'Fred Ives', and coral aloes.

Orchestrating the Ideal Site for Succulents

Because they are the least demanding of all plants, succulents require very little from their owners. However, for succulents to look their best, they do need some consideration as you're laying out your site. Imagine being rooted and unable to move, and then exposed to too much (or too little) light, wind, heat, rain, and cold. Landscape professionals and gardening enthusiasts who use succulents as a living palette make a point of providing the right sun exposure, microclimates, and soil mix.

Which way is the sun?

Every so often a homeowner surprises me by being uncertain where north is. Yet I admit that when I took possession of my yard more than two decades ago, I wasn't sure either. I've since learned that orientation to the sun is a key factor in garden design and plant placement. Sun is essential for photosynthesis, which gives plants energy needed for growth and flowering. Although any succulent's optimal sun exposure depends on numerous factors (among them the type of plant, whether it's newly introduced to the garden, and if it's actively growing or dormant), the rule of thumb is to locate a succulent garden where it will receive five or six hours of direct sun daily and bright shade for the remainder. As it happens, my sloping garden faces east. Plants bask in gentle morning sun and are in shade during the heat of the afternoon—a nice bonus for them and for me as well.

Also notice how the intensity, duration, and even location of the sun's rays change gradually throughout the seasons. As your pinpoint on the planet rotates toward or away from the sun during the year, sunrise and sunset occur earlier or later and at slightly different places on the horizon. An area that is fully shaded in winter might have significantly more sun in summer and vice versa.

Rosette succulents (such as aeoniums and echeverias) grown in too little light will flatten to expose more

If these succulents could speak, they'd say, "The sun is over there!"

of their leaf surface to the sun. This, and when a plant becomes elongated from seeking sunlight, is called *etiolation*. If the plant is in a pot, rotating it 180 degrees once a week or so helps prevent lopsided growth.

The sun also impacts a garden's aesthetics. Sunlight cast on spiny plants makes them glow and creates intriguing shadows. Silhouettes and the sky are part of a landscape, as is the wind, which creates motion.

Narrow-leaved succulents such as *Yucca rostrata* are kinetic sculptures that shimmer when sunlit and ripple in the breeze.

Match the plant to the microclimate

My half-acre garden is in one of San Diego's inland valleys, which tend to be several degrees colder in winter than surrounding hilltops. Frost-tender plants such as avocados, palms, and bougainvilleas, common elsewhere in the region, are seldom grown in these low-lying areas. Cold air, being heavier than warm, flows downward and pools. Most seasonal frosts are mild, so only leaf tips freeze, making the plants look singed—hence the term *frost burn*.

My across-the-street neighbors are slightly higher in elevation and give frost little thought. When it's 30°F down in my garden, it's a degree or two *above* freezing in theirs. For succulents such as kalanchoes, crassulas, and many euphorbias, a few degrees below freezing can mean death or deformity. If they're exposed to 32°F or lower long enough, moisture in their tissues solidifies, expands, and bursts cell walls. Those few degrees also mean that their owner has to dash around covering them with bedsheets when a lingering frost is

Agave americana in Jim Bishop's steep north-facing garden leans in the direction of greatest sun exposure.

All great gardens are light-and-shadow experiences, and Alex Geremia's is no exception. The tree aloe is 'Hercules', the blue explosions with trunks, *Yucca rostrata*.

predicted—unless, of course, they're already growing in the garden's warmer microclimates.

A microclimate in your garden is any area with a distinct set of growing conditions that differ from those of your overall property. To identify your garden's cold pockets, notice where ice crystals linger the longest after sunrise. Warm spots tend to be near boulders, structures, trees, hardscape, and asphalt, all of which absorb heat from the sun. Your garden's warmest area, and the best place to grow frost-tender succulents in winter, is likely to be south facing—such as a slope backed by a fence or retaining wall.

Wind is a factor, too. Garden areas shielded by walls, hedges, or some other windbreak are warmer than those out in the open. Locations exposed to northerly winds tend to be colder. But wind isn't always a problem; air that moves is less of a threat than air that's still, because movement keeps cold air from settling around plants. Wind can make leaves more frost resistant because it has a drying effect, and drier leaves contain less water. Good air circulation also discourages pests and fungal diseases, to which succulents are prone in damp climates. Excessive wind will cause desiccation, however, and if you're sheltering your plants within a cold frame, in a greenhouse, or beneath a cover, wind may cause greater heat loss by cooling the air around the structure.

Tree canopies, by providing bright shade in summer and a barrier against cold in winter, moderate the temperature beneath them, thereby shielding understory plants from both sunburn and frost.

What roots want you to know

Although succulents aren't fussy about soil, their lives depend on good drainage. Determine your garden soil's consistency by digging a hole the size of a 1-gallon nursery pot and then filling the hole with water. If it drains in a few minutes or less, the soil is probably sandy and will benefit from the addition of organic matter. If the

TOP *Aeonium* 'Zwartkop' and *Euphorbia tirucalli* 'Sticks on Fire' benefit from warmth radiated from boulders on frosty nights.

BOTTOM At the Huntington Botanical Gardens in San Marino, California, hundred-year-old *Aloe barberae* trees create a beneficial microclimate for *Agave attenuata*, *Aloe petricola*, and *Aeonium* 'Zwartkop'.

A palo verde tree at the Ruth Bancroft Garden in Walnut Creek, California, is in full bloom, its fallen petals forming delicate yellow drifts. The tree's canopy protects succulents underneath it from too much sun in summer and frost in winter—as does the structure at upper right.

water takes an hour or more to drain, the soil likely is clay and inhospitable to succulents—indeed, to most garden plants—because waterlogged roots may rot. If you have heavy clay soil that drains poorly, you might want to remove it and replace it with a commercial cactus mix. Or simply plant in good soil mounded above the existing soil, or construct planters atop it—that is, raised beds. Made of block, stone, or pressure-treated wood, these function like large pots.

Since soil varies from region to region, and even within areas of a garden, amendment formulas vary. In general, though, succulents planted in average garden soils benefit from having the soil amended with equal parts crushed lava rock (pumice), organic matter (humus or compost), and coarse sand (like decomposed granite).

BELOW To appreciate the difference a topdressing makes, imagine this newly installed garden without it. Rock colors were chosen to harmonize with the home's exterior and with terraces constructed from granite boulders found on-site. Like shadows cast by clouds, patches of gray-toned gravel contrast with sunnier-hued crushed rock.

RIGHT Planters contain good soil, elevate succulents for better viewing and ease of maintenance, and protect them from active dogs, kids, and anything on wheels. Low stone walls double as benches. Succulents include a statuesque *Aloe marlothii* (right), crimson-flowered *Kalanchoe blossfeldiana* (foreground), and a cluster of *Euphorbia resinifera*.

Pumice aerates the soil, absorbs excess moisture, and provides plants with micronutrients.

Also called sharp sand, coarse sand—unlike fine, silty sand—has grains that feel sharp when rubbed between the fingertips. Succulents generally prefer slightly acidic soil (pH between 6 and 7).

Botanical gardens, like homeowners, contend with native soil that's not ideal for cacti and succulents, and amend it accordingly. At the Ruth Bancroft Garden in Walnut Creek, California, for example, rocky soil is used to build up mounds atop the existing clay, with lots of pumice added beneath the more sensitive plants, and compost used as mulch. At the Huntington Botanical Gardens in San Marino near Los Angeles, forest compost is added to the soil, plus pumice if drainage needs improvement. Heavy soil at the Arizona-Sonora Desert Museum in Tucson, which showcases cacti, is topped with 6 to 12 inches of well-draining soil mixed with enough sulfur to keep the pH between 6.5 and 8.

The only definitive method to find out which additives—such as agricultural lime and compost—will turn your soil into the perfect growing medium is to analyze it. Large nurseries, garden centers, and home improvement stores sell soil pH test kits. Your local agricultural advisories and Master Gardener associations can also provide guidance.

What goes on top of the soil is important, too. Inorganic topdressings—as opposed to wood chips and shredded bark—are best for succulents because they don't harbor pests and diseases, nor do they keep the plants' crowns overly moist. Moreover, organic topdressings break down over time and have to be reapplied. Crushed rock, available in a variety of colors and sizes at garden centers and landscape suppliers, offers aesthetic as well as practical advantages. By covering bare dirt it lends a finished look, and when applied to a depth of several inches, it keeps sunlight from the soil, thereby discouraging weeds from sprouting (and if they do, they're easier to pull). Gravel also absorbs the sun's warmth, allows rain to percolate into the soil, reduces evaporation, and keeps the ground insulated, thereby promoting root growth. In general, the darker the rock, the more heat it absorbs.

Mexican fence post cacti (*Pachycereus marginatus*) are in proportion with this stone wall and need no more room for their roots than the narrow bed along its base. They also illustrate the principle of repetition in an obvious way; more subtly, their bold forms contrast with the wall's color and texture. Notice, too, how the overall design emphasizes the archway.

Stone pilasters and urns in Jeanne Meadow's garden in Fallbrook, California, are the right size for a dramatic pair of *Furcraea macdougalii* (related to agave, native to Mexico, cold hardy to the mid-20s F). Spilling from the pots is *Senecio radicans*.

LEFT Large pots are well worth the investment when they significantly enhance a home's ambience and architecture. These are in scale with the home's entry, make the area appear more upscale and inviting, and elevate colorful plants to eye level.

Six Design Must-Dos for a Great-Looking Garden

Most people love bright colors, which is why gardens in bloom are so appealing. But color is only one aspect of design, and other elements are equally important. Most of us notice the others subliminally. Learn to recognize them, and you'll be well on your way to creating aesthetically pleasing container compositions, garden vignettes (composed arrangements designed to enhance a particular setting), and even entire landscapes. Whenever you see a garden that makes you want to linger but you don't know why, analyze it. Chances are, it exemplifies one or more of six design essentials: scale and proportion, repetition, contrast, emphasis, shape and texture, and color.

Scale and proportion

Scale and proportion have to do with the size of plants and structures in the landscape as they relate to one another and to the whole. A landscape with properly proportioned elements feels inviting and is a good fit for its human inhabitants. For example, a large tree looks proportional alongside a multistory building but would dwarf a small house. A 3-foot pond that suits a small yard would be lost in a large park. Correct scale and proportion can be as simple as placing small plants in small spaces and big plants in large spaces. Generally, it's more effective to fill a blank wall or corner with a single dasylirion—or a large ornamental pot—than a jumble of, say, geraniums.

Intimate areas lend themselves to frilly echeverias and jewel-like sedums; large areas, to majestic agaves, yuccas, and aloes, and companion plants such as phormiums, cycads, and ornamental grasses. If your backyard feels open and unprotected, the right-size plants can transform it into a sheltered outdoor room. Conversely, an area of your yard that feels claustrophobic will benefit from removing clutter and pruning overgrown trees and shrubs.

A large pot's smooth, rounded surface contrasts with the sharply pointed leaves of 'Blue Glow' agaves. At the same time, the vessel repeats the agaves' spherical rosettes, which in turn have translucent leaf margins the same color as the pot.

A turquoise-glazed pot calls attention to the similarly colored leaves of *Echeveria subrigida*, as do bits of turquoise glass in the topdressing. The red edges of the leaves lend contrast.

Aloe mitriformis (foreground) and *A. capitata* have color and form in common yet also incorporate contrasts of the same.

Repetition

Perhaps more than any other plants, succulents—because their leaf shapes are distinctly pointed, oval, or cylindrical—offer opportunities for crisply defined repetitions of form.

Repetition can be a difficult principle for plant collectors who want one of everything and see no point in having more than one of anything. But repetition is essential for unifying a landscape. Large agaves, in particular, illustrate this: just three of them, all the same and strategically placed, will lend continuity to a garden regardless of its other components. And if those agaves are variegated, so much the better; their striped leaves provide another motif.

Repetition is not always multiples of the same plant. There are subtler ways to achieve it, such as with patterns, textures, and silhouettes. A yucca planted near an agave shares the same spiky shape, as do tufts of blue fescue at its base. Colors, too, are an effective way of playing the same tune with multiple instruments.

To visually expand this pocket garden beyond its physical parameters, designer Laura Eubanks used golden jade to echo a yellow euonymus shrub on the opposite side of the path.

ABOVE A massed planting of *Agave* 'Blue Flame' effectively illustrates the plant's name (pointed, wavy leaves overlap to create repetitions that suggest flames). Echeveria and aloe blooms flanking the agaves provide contrasting texture and color.

OPPOSITE Bayonet leaves of *Agave angustifolia* 'Marginata' repeat in the plants' starburst shapes, which in turn share the same shades of green and cream as finer-textured *Portulacaria afra* 'Variegata'. The portulacaria's lacy form adds contrast, as do its stems—red is the color complement of green. Repeating the agaves enhances the composition, too.

In the aptly named Garden of Contrasts at Cornerstone Gardens in Sonoma, California, wispy Mexican feather grass (*Nassella tenuissima*) provides yin to the yang of large agaves. Notice, too, the finer texture of the olive trees and the large ball in the background, which adds a touch of whimsy and serves as a focal point.

The designer selected the boulder for its burnt-orange tones, then planted *Euphorbia tirucalli* 'Sticks on Fire' to echo its color and provide contrasting texture. Sunset jade also lends contrasting color and texture while repeating the boulder's shape.

At Seaside Gardens nursery in Carpinteria, California, *Agave attenuata* (blue variety), red-flowered *Euphorbia milii*, and yellow-green *Crassula ovata* 'Gollum' contrast with each other in color, texture, and form.

Contrast

If repetition is soothing, contrast is exciting. As shown previously, well-designed gardens often have both. Repetition by itself is effective up to a point and then becomes tedious, which is when contrast comes into play. For example, in a multiple planting of agaves and yuccas, the addition of airy ornamental grasses is refreshing. Or you might add a succulent that contrasts with the agaves' blue-gray, such as an orange aloe or a red crassula.

Asymmetry, a form of contrast, is useful for relieving monotony. Although symmetry—such as urns planted with aeoniums flanking an entryway, or a driveway bordered on both sides with aloes—can be pleasing because of repetition, few plants in nature form perfect pairs or rows. Anything aligned, straight, or right-angled speaks of human intervention. Asymmetry, with its irregular curves and odd numbers, is natural.

A serpentine pathway that disappears into the garden creates a sense of mystery. What do you suppose lies beyond that curve?

Designer Michael Buckner used a euphorbia that branches from its base to call attention to distant skyscrapers, thereby bringing the San Diego skyline into a client's garden across the bay.

In Claire Chao's Honolulu garden, Madagascar palm (*Pachypodium lamerei*) and aloes lead the eye upward, emphasizing the view. Rooftops, aloe flowers, and rock topdressing—all red-orange—contrast with blue ocean and sky.

Emphasis

Any item strategically placed to attract attention, such as a tree, statue, or fountain used as a focal point, provides the essential element of emphasis. Hardscape and fences, intentionally or not, create sight lines that lead the eye to what lies beyond. A bend in a pathway or a view-embracing gap in a hedge do so as well. Use such aspects of your garden to call attention to specific focal points and destinations, such as sitting areas, gates, doorways, plant vignettes, or an inviting allée.

Take photos of your garden. You'll be amazed how easy it is to evaluate focal points and sight lines when they're framed by a camera lens. What an area needs may suddenly become obvious—such as removing or concealing a too-prominent plant or object.

If you live on a slope overlooking a city skyline, distant mountains, the ocean, or a verdant canyon, position sitting and entertaining areas accordingly and design the garden to emphasize the view. Your home's windows also call attention to the outdoors beyond. If a view offers something pleasing and framing it isn't an option, repeat the far-off item's shape or color in the foreground.

Illuminate your garden at night for aesthetics as well as safety. Low-voltage lighting that brightens pathways and stairs isn't difficult to install and is an effective way to emphasize statuesque succulents. By transforming your garden into a nighttime gallery of sculptural plants, you'll experience a new appreciation of their forms and textures, and so will your neighbors and guests.

ABOVE Similar to *Agave franzosinii*, large blue A. 'Sawtooth' (upper right) is a guaranteed attention grabber. Below it is *Aloe rubroviolacea*, and at lower right, *Agave geminiflora*. Tall red-stemmed shrubs are *Portulacaria afra*.

OPPOSITE At dusk, low-voltage lights in a San Diego garden come on automatically. They're positioned to emphasize bold succulents such as these dragon trees (*Dracaena draco*).

Another useful landscaping concept is the axis, a visual line that extends between two emphasized elements, such as a walkway that connects sitting areas. In formal gardens, plants are typically aligned on either side of an axis, and focal points are positioned where two axes intersect.

Sight lines also can point to undesirable objects, so evaluate your landscape for unattractive items you have seen so often you no longer see them. One way to gain fresh perspective on your garden is to turn your back on it and look at its reflection in a handheld mirror. When I did that in my own yard, I noticed a yellow road sign on the busy street beyond. Before I saw the sign reflected in the mirror, I had been oblivious to it.

When you identify an eyesore, take measures to make it less obvious. Either position something intriguing in the same line of sight so the viewer's eye stops there or camouflage the offending object with shrubs or a structure, such as a lattice screen. If the problem is a telephone pole, a vertical plant will help hide it and draw the eye away from it. Conversely, avoid repeating prominent elements of an eyesore, lest you make it stand out even more; the eye has a tendency to bounce back and forth between similar objects. White patio furniture, for example, may visually add a neighbor's white boat or van to your garden.

Should you want to veil neighboring second-story windows, add lacy trees that have cultivation requirements similar to succulents but that are much faster growing, such as melaleuca, palo verde, or acacia. Multiple plantings of yuccas, *Euphorbia tirucalli*, *Portulacaria afra* (elephant's food), *Pedilanthus bracteatus* (lady's slipper plant), *Aloe arborescens*, opuntias, and agaves can also serve as living walls, screens, and hedges.

After a yellow street sign jumped out at me from beyond my garden, I planted a tree to conceal it and added a focal point to draw the eye away from it. The sign is at left, amid the foliage.

Shape and texture

You may find it easier to repeat and contrast succulents of all sorts if you think of them as shapes or silhouettes. Large agaves resemble fountains; small ones, artichokes. Dasylirions and certain yuccas and agaves are pincushions. Aloes suggest spiders, octopuses, or sea stars. Cacti are paddles, globes, or columns; aeoniums, daisies; echeverias, roses; and sedums are beads, bullets, or beans.

Texture, which is visual as well as tactile, is integral to other elements of design and refers to the way light hits surfaces. Use texture to enhance contrast and repetition and to create or call attention to focal points. Keep it in mind as you select and position plants that have fuzzy, waxy, shiny, or dull leaves. Other textural aspects of a garden include tree bark, roof tiles, rocks and hardscape, and the overall shapes and forms of shrubs—which can change depending on whether they're viewed up close or from a distance. Textural effects are relative to their surroundings. Even gravel, which at first appears coarse, can look soft when placed alongside boulders.

ABOVE Textures, colors, and shapes repeat and contrast in a composition that includes tawny *Euphorbia tirucalli* 'Sticks on Fire', blue *Senecio serpens*, and butter-yellow barrel cacti (*Echinocactus grusonii*).

RIGHT, TOP At Chanticleer, a public garden near Philadelphia, a hardy cactus (*Opuntia humifusa*) massed with yellow flowers contrasts in shape and texture with the blue fescue behind it. Gravel adds texture, enhances drainage, and hides bare soil.

RIGHT, BOTTOM A pair of *Dasylirion longissimum* specimens resemble wide-open sprinklers, lending great texture to a streetside garden in Rancho Santa Fe, California. In this layered landscape, *Euphorbia milii* flowers echo bougainvillea bracts, and *Senecio mandraliscae* forms a blanket of blue.

A three-plant combo of succulents effectively contrasts the textures of pointed-leaved yuccas, oval opuntia paddles, and conical aloe flowers. Repetition occurs in similarly shaped plants, multiple cactus pads, and orange blooms.

Color

Succulents with colorful leaves are the celebrities of the plant world and the darlings of garden designers. People invariably notice a plant with unusual foliage color, be it bronze, blue, silver, gray, crimson, yellow, chartreuse, lavender, or variegated.

Because succulents come in such glorious colors, you might expect the flowers to play second fiddle, but they blaze in hues even brighter than the leaves. Flowers on thick stems tend to be long lasting, both on the plants and in bouquets. Because their fleshy stems hold moisture, the blooms of many succulents—among them aloes, aeoniums, echeverias, and kalanchoes—will stay fresh for a week or more in a vase without water. In fact, the addition of water may cause stems to soften prematurely.

Grown en masse, succulents with colorful foliage make an unforgettable display. Solo, they serve as the centerpiece of a potted arrangement or as garden focal points. And when a colorful succulent is juxtaposed with other boldly hued plants or objects, the contrast is as dramatic as it is delightful.

Some succulents, such as the blue senecios, retain their foliage color regardless of their growing conditions. Others, including most crassulas and many aloes

BELOW In a Bonsall, California, garden, tuxedo agaves (*Agave americana* 'Mediopicta Alba') contrast with crassulas in bloom, orange *Euphorbia tirucalli* 'Sticks on Fire', purple-hued cotyledons, and 'Sunburst' aeoniums.

BOTTOM Overlapping leaves of *Crassula rupestris* repeat the pot's blue-and-orange glaze. Hints of green in the glaze echo the red-edged jade (*C. ovata* 'Crosby's Compact') and coppertone stonecrop (*Sedum nussbaumerianum*).

Orange firesticks and a blue senecio are perfect alongside an azure pool with terra-cotta-colored coping.

ABOVE Silver *Agave titanota*, despite its comparatively pale leaves, upstages burgundy *Crassula pubescens*, *Aeonium* 'Sunburst', sunset jade, and coppertone stonecrop. In the background are variegated *Agave attenuata*, red *Aloe cameronii*, and magenta-and-teal *Kalanchoe luciae* 'Fantastic'. Dark green hedgehog agaves (*Agave stricta*) mirror each other while contrasting with the rest of the composition.

RIGHT A potted arrangement combines rosette succulents in shades of coral, pink, teal, and purple—*Graptopetalum paraguayense*, *Echeveria* 'Afterglow', and ×*Graptosedum* 'California Sunset'—as well as a good companion plant for succulents, *Tradescantia pallida* 'Purpurea' at lower left.

and sedums, turn from green to shades of rose, red, and orange when grown in full sun or stressed by cold or drought. (See the sidebar on stressing succulents for color in "Success Secrets for Succulents.")

Swaths of color are more effective than blotches, and any color is enhanced by its complement (complementary colors include blue and orange, yellow and purple, red and green). When pairing colors, use them in roughly equal amounts to create a balanced composition. Add a third to bring out the other two—such as chartreuse with orange and blue.

The more vivid the contrast, the more memorable the composition, but complementary colors need not be the same intensity. For example, try pairing a peach-colored plant with deep purple, or pale gold with lavender. Mix all sorts of colors but avoid blending cool and warm reds or pairing blue-gray succulents with cobalt or royal blue containers; such combinations seldom look right together.

Hot hues jump out at the viewer, while greens and blues tend to recede. Use yellow, cream, and chartreuse to brighten shady spots, and red and orange to add punch to areas viewed from a distance. If a part of your garden seems too hot and bright, cool it with plants in shades of green, such as clusters of *Aeonium canariense*, *Cotyledon orbiculata*, or *Agave attenuata*.

At dusk or by moonlight, pale gray foliage appears to glow. Silvery gray agaves, cotyledons, and kalanchoes are refreshing yet dramatic when combined with succulents with hot-hued leaves. For great color and texture contrast, plant *Artemisia* 'Powis Castle'—a low-water, woody perennial with lacy gray leaves—alongside burgundy-black *Aeonium* 'Zwartkop', gold-bronze *Sedum nussbaumerianum*, yellow jade (*Crassula ovata* 'Hummel's Sunset'), or any red-orange aloe.

Color, the diva of design elements, can overshadow the others and make discerning them difficult. Typically this happens when you're trying to evaluate a tired garden in need of refurbishing. Bay Area garden designer Rebecca Sweet recommends taking a photo of the area, then printing it in black and white. When you see the garden in terms of essential aspects of design other than color—repetition, contrast, scale and proportion, shape and texture, and emphasis—what's needed becomes evident.

Kalanchoe tomentosa 'Chocolate Soldier' is one of the few brown-leaved succulents. Its cinnamon-silver tones pair effectively with a well-stressed aloe and yellow *Sedum adolphi*. The kalanchoe's fuzzy leaves also lend textural contrast.

In a Santa Barbara garden, *Crassula capitella* 'Campfire' holds its own with brilliant bougainvilleas.

A copper-colored fountain serves as a Bay Area garden's glistening focal point. Repeating its orange hue are the edges of *Agave* 'Blue Glow' and *Sedum ×rubrotinctum* 'Pork and Beans'—which also offer contrasting textures. In the background are *Senecio vitalis* and euphorbia shrubs.

Enhancing Your Succulent Showplace

As you conceptualize your landscape, consider incorporating enhancements that make your garden an inviting extension of your home. Options include birdbaths and water features; colorful walls; a structure such as a potting shed, gazebo, or greenhouse; art objects; and outdoor furniture such as benches, chairs, a dining table, chaise lounges, and patio umbrellas.

Water features and dry creek beds

Any garden benefits from the addition of water, real or suggested. Splashing water blankets intrusive sounds

Adirondack chairs painted light blue make same-colored succulents (in particular, *Senecio mandraliscae*) stand out.

In designer Laura Eubanks's Eastlake, California, backyard, a small waterfall and pond provide soothing sounds and reflections. Green aeoniums growing alongside them echo the green ovals of lily pads, and several sizes of rounded stones repeat the pond's circular shape. Its bottom isn't visible, giving the illusion of greater depth and volume of water than is actually there.

ABOVE Provide a water source for birds and butterflies by extending a drip tube to a rock basin and concealing the emitter with plants. The basin will fill whenever your automatic irrigation system runs.

RIGHT Although it's in a residential yard, this dry creek looks like it might be in the backcountry. Amid half-buried boulders grow *Aloe arborescens* and annual wildflowers.

ABOVE A dry creek bed dug well below grade and lined with boulders appears to have been carved by rushing water.

ABOVE, RIGHT In a Coronado, California, backyard, a rock whirlpool seems to flow into the bay. The cobbles are naturally smooth from tumbling in water, and installing them on their sides enhances the illusion of rapid flow.

and muffles conversations so even your closest neighbors can't overhear. It also mirrors the sky, creates a habitat for fish and birds, and sparkles beautifully in sunlight.

Fountains need a water source, a catch basin, and electricity to run a recirculating pump. To help a fountain appear integral to its surroundings, conceal its basin with stones and plants.

In parched regions, the need to conserve water inspires garden enhancements that merely suggest its presence. Dry creek beds hint that water flows during the rainy season. Riverlike swales of rounded rocks and gravel not only lend visual interest, they can also serve to channel rainwater from gutters into the garden.

Rather than having a dry stream extend from wall to pavement, design it with a plausible beginning and end. Use ornamental grasses that resemble reeds to conceal aspects of the bed that might detract from the illusion. Install the dry creek below ground level—as though it had been formed by erosion—and partially bury rocks that define it. If you merely place stones atop the soil, you'll end up with an unnatural serpentine pile.

In Hannah and Howard Jarson's garden, boulders and cobbles line a swale that suggests a seasonal creek, doubles as a pathway, and leads the eye to the garden and view beyond. Arching over the dry streambed are lacy melaleuca (paperbark) trees.

Succulent-planted fountains

Water exposed to warm, dry air evaporates quickly, which is one reason owners of tiered fountains in dry climates opt to turn off the pump—it's a waste of water. An aesthetically intriguing alternative is to plant the fountain with succulents. The ideal location is in bright shade, dappled sun, or morning sun only. (This is also true for succulent-planted birdbaths.) As with any nondraining container, as long as their roots don't sit in soggy soil—which promotes the growth of pathogens—the plants will be fine. Use a porous mix of half potting soil and half pumice, which absorbs excess moisture, and make sure succulents sharing a basin have similar cultivation requirements.

Succulents that cascade and suggest dripping water include rosary vine (*Ceropegia woodii*), *Senecio jacobsenii*, and numerous trailing sedums with foliage that ranges from fine textured to bullet shaped. Good for zones 4 to 9 is stringy stonecrop (*Sedum sarmentosum*), which is hardy to –30°F and thrives in full sun to part shade. String of pearls (*Senecio rowleyanus*) has spherical leaves that resemble water drops, but it may turn into a string of dried peas in full, hot sun. Unless you live in a mild maritime climate, grow it in bright shade. A tougher alternative when it comes to sun and heat is string of bananas (*Senecio radicans*).

Senecio radicans (string of bananas) pours over the top tier; *Sedum burrito*, the middle. Large echeverias need no raison d'être, but they do suggest circles made by droplets on the surface of water. If this were your planted fountain, would you snip those flower spikes?

Sedum sarmentosum splashes over the sides of Ada Davidson's dry fountain in Sewickley, Pennsylvania. Basins painted purple add whimsy; and they contrast with the sedum's bright chartreuse.

Colorful walls, practical structures, and inviting pathways

When you choose your home's color or paint a shed or fence, think beyond traditional tan, beige, and white. Warm hues of yellow, ochre, and rose make dramatic contrasting backdrops for succulents; muted greens provide soothing repetitions, and there's nothing quite like royal blue. If you lack the courage or energy to repaint your entire house, do one exterior wall. This involves little expense or time, and if you don't like it, you can repaint it.

ABOVE Patrick Anderson painted a garden wall royal blue as a backdrop for aloes that bloom in midwinter. Mexican fence post (*Pachycereus marginatus*) and other succulents look good with it, too.

RIGHT Tumbling over a yellow-painted retaining wall are *Aloe ciliaris* and *Kalanchoe marnieriana*, both in bloom. *Aloe* 'Hercules' dominates the garden behind them. Purple statice (*Limonium perezii*) is at upper right.

Patrick Anderson tested several shades of green and orange before he picked these for his entry. You might call them *Euphorbia ammak* 'Variegata' green and *Sedum nussbaumerianum* orange—or not.

OPPOSITE, LEFT The exterior of designer Gabriel Frank's home is the same soft blue-green as his succulents, including a majestic *Agave* 'Mr. Ripple'. Peach-colored topdressing is the perfect complement.

OPPOSITE, RIGHT A peach-pink wall repeats the sunset hue of *Euphorbia tirucalli* 'Sticks on Fire', which in turn contrasts with the gray-blue ornamental grass and *Cotyledon orbiculata* (lower right). Shapes contrast: the euphorbia in the background is tall and slender, 'Sticks on Fire' is midsize and shrubby, and *Festuca glauca* forms a low mass of upthrusting points.

Outdoor living areas enhance your enjoyment of your home, extend it into your garden, and maximize the value and use of your land. For example, when positioned outside a sliding glass door, a patio or deck provides an easily accessible dining and sitting area. Situated in the garden—perhaps alongside a pool or barbecue grill—such areas serve as outdoor rooms. To make them inviting at night, install a fire pit or outdoor fireplace plus low-voltage lighting that automatically comes on at dusk.

If you have small children, you may want to set aside areas for a lawn, sandbox, and swing set. Keep in mind that bright-colored plastic jungle gyms and aging playhouses can become eyesores, so don't position them prominently.

Trellises and arbors are instant focal points that lend height and interest to any landscape. Depending on their location, such structures might divide two outdoor areas, support a flowering vine, or frame a sheltered destination. Position one near a gathering area, and friends may ask if your garden is available for weddings.

Gabions (empty cubes made of heavy gauge wire) can serve as modular building blocks for outdoor structures. The cubes, which have a contemporary, industrial look, can be stacked to create walls or pedestals, or placed side by side for seating. Gabions can be completely or partially filled with anything weatherproof; they generally hold ornamental stones that serve as ballast, but weight could also be provided by repurposed objects such as bricks (which look good stacked

At the Desert Botanical Garden in Phoenix, sun sails provide welcome shade for plants and visitors alike.

A raised deck and sitting area, sheltered by a pergola that holds a hundred-year-old wisteria vine, incorporates a pizza oven and an outdoor fireplace. When viewed from the garden, the area serves as both focal point and destination.

An archway flanked by succulents announces the entrance to a garden in San Luis Obispo, California.

For their award-winning display at the San Francisco Flower and Garden Show, designers Eric Arneson and Nahal Sohbati of the Academy of Art University created an open-air room walled with gabions containing rounded stones that suggest a sloping rock wall. A bench of vertical 4-by-4s also consists of squares. Behind the designers, succulents inserted horizontally into the wire mesh while still in their nursery pots create a vertical garden.

ABOVE Golden decomposed granite top-dresses bare dirt and flows around islandlike raised beds. Pavers set into the DG repeat the rust hues of boulders that rim the beds and retain the soil within them.

BELOW Gravel is inexpensive, permeable, and easy to install, and it stays put. Because it crunches when stepped on, it also announces visitors and discourages trespassers.

diagonally in a diamond pattern). Place a container-grown plant inside a gabion, and its stems and leaves will grow through the openings. A higher-end option is to fill the wire cubes with chunks of glass and illuminate them at night. They can also be left empty to let in sunlight and air.

Pathways are aesthetic enhancements to a garden that provide firm footing, connect various areas, serve as access routes for anything with wheels, and bring aeoniums, aloes, echeverias, and more up close. The best-looking pathways are paved with bricks, stone, gravel, stamped concrete, or decomposed granite (DG)—the most popular walkway material after concrete and asphalt. My garden's pathways are gravel, flagstone, and decomposed granite. The last is natural looking, comparatively inexpensive, and permeable so rain or overspray aren't wasted; it can be stabilized to reduce erosion and mud.

A brick walkway through the aloe garden at Ganna Walska Lotusland in Montecito, California, is an art form underfoot. Its labor-intensive pattern dates to the 1920s.

A life-size sculpture by Phillip Glashoff in Alex Geremia's garden near Santa Barbara appears to dance with joy.

TOP Sculptor John Robinson constructed this life-size figure of St. Francis of Assisi from scrap metal, for daughter Cindy Evans and her husband Mark's garden in Laguna Beach, California. Behind the sculpture is a stand of minimally spined opuntia.

BOTTOM A fan-shaped sculpture made of metal pipes suits the contemporary architecture of a Los Gatos, California, home. Flanking the bold, stylized agave are blue echeverias (*Echeveria imbricata*) that resemble cabbage roses.

Outdoor art, alive and otherwise

The architectural and sculptural qualities of agaves and other large succulents make them wonderful backdrops for art objects. Creating an outdoor gallery will enhance your enjoyment of your garden, make it more memorable and interesting, and give you an incentive to collect and display beautiful things. As to what "art" might be, the answer is anything weatherproof you find tasteful and would enjoy seeing daily.

If you're uncertain how to select art for your garden, consider your home's architecture. Rustic objects may look out of place if the house is contemporary, and vice versa. Victorian birdhouses, floral flags, and bunnies—anything fussy, darling, or cute—are better suited to the flowerbeds of a cottage garden than to a setting dominated by the bold drama of large agaves or the simple elegance of columnar cacti. To unify your selections, each piece of art might include a color, material, theme, or style found in the others. Or you might collect and display works by the same artist.

In general, try to avoid clichés and most things mass produced. If you must add something seen often, like a planted wheelbarrow or a gazing globe, display it in such a way that it illustrates your individual style. Your garden is unlike any other, as are you, so aim to create what no one else has. Also limit the number of objects. Once you become a collector of outdoor art, your garden is at risk for clutter. Less is more, so if need be, replace existing items with recent acquisitions and store any you can't part with.

Art objects ideally are in scale with their surroundings and contrast with or repeat other aspects of the garden. When placing an assortment of small objects,

A mosaic of an agave transformed an eyesore—the base of a light pole—into the focal point of a vignette at the Water Conservation Garden in El Cajon, California.

One of many tipped pots at the Denver Botanic Gardens appears to spill its contents—*Delosperma* 'Kelaidis'. Forming a feathery backdrop is the ornamental grass *Panicum virgatum*.

Louisa Campagna lives near the San Diego Zoo, and recently a hippo by a visiting artist surfaced in her succulent garden. (All that's visible is its bristly muzzle.) Surrounding the metal sculpture are *Lampranthus deltoides*, sunset jade, *Euphorbia tirucalli* 'Sticks on Fire', *E. milii*, and variegated aeoniums.

give them greater presence by grouping them. Set intricate pieces near sitting areas so they can be appreciated close-up; put larger ones where they're visible from a distance. Don't simply locate them along pathways; attach them to fences, hang them from tree branches, and set them atop boulders or pedestals.

To test whether decorative objects or outdoor furnishings enhance, detract from, or have minimal impact on the settings you've selected, live with them a few days. Sooner or later you'll become so engrossed in gardening you'll forget they're there and come upon them afresh. Do they delight or disappoint you? Seem just right, irrelevant, redundant, or trite? Do the colors work?

Inform guests that an art piece is on trial and ask their honest opinions. (This is not the time to regale

them with stories of how much you love it and what a great deal you got.) If you're still uncertain, remove the item and see if you miss it. If not, here's what I do: attempt to return it, try to persuade a grown child to take it, donate it, or stash it in the basement.

Sophisticated whimsy

Decorative objects and garden vignettes not only express your individuality, creativity, and cleverness but can also convey your sense of humor. When done well, sophisticated whimsy transforms visitors into eager children, fascinated and fully in the moment, keen to discover more. Of course, what delights one person may dismay another. Coming across a planted urinal in a garden may make some guests laugh out loud and others

A gazing globe in a succulent-planted fountain suggests a bubble, glints in the sun, and reflects its surroundings.

A pot with a regal furcraea headdress reigns over a garden of succulents, barrel cacti, and broad-leaved tropical trees.

gamely pretend to be amused. If kindred spirits are those delighted by your wit, this might be one way to find them.

Intriguing yet inexpensive objects that have the potential for refined whimsy and work well with the shapes and symmetry of succulents can be found at architectural and industrial salvage suppliers. Even metal car parts can be given a new life as containers for succulents, causing visitors to pause and ask, "What is that?"

The downside to rusty or dark-colored items is that they tend to disappear when positioned in the shade or against a backdrop of mottled foliage. They're better in silhouette, with the sky or a wall behind them, or painted a light color. In my garden, several wire sculptures blended in, so I primed them with rustproof paint and then spray-painted them yellow. The items now are clearly visible and repeat a color elsewhere in the garden. If adding a wire insect to your garden, paint the body a light color but leave unpainted the metal rod attached to it. The bug will appear airborne.

I like ornamental lizards that make guests do a double take. This one, in the garden of J Bassage and Shelley Vinatieri, nearly went home with me.

OPPOSITE A cow skeleton in cactus collector Larry Nichols's front yard is probably unprecedented in his Orange County, California, housing development.

Transforming Your Front Yard with Succulents

You and your neighbors see your front yard daily, so it's important to do it right. Curb appeal also increases your home's value. Traditional front yard landscapes tend to be bland and high maintenance, with turf that needs mowing, fertilizing, and dethatching. Lawns are often bordered by shrubs that need pruning and beds planted with annuals that must be replaced. Trees drop leaves that require raking. No green component will survive without regular and ample water.

Envision instead a meandering pathway of brick or stone that connects the sidewalk to your front door. Flanking it are berms dotted with boulders and planted with aeoniums, agaves, echeverias, and tree aloes. Ice plants and ornamental grasses provide contrasting colors and textures.

When you redo a front yard that's level (or nearly so), you have the option of creating highs and lows that suggest hills and valleys. Mounded soil is more visually interesting, adds instant height to young trees, and discourages people and pets from cutting across newly planted areas. A valley between berms can serve as a pathway, suggest a dry streambed, or lead to a side-yard gate or tucked-away sitting area. Because succulents tend to be shallow rooted (seldom deeper than 12 inches except for tree varieties), berms needn't be high. However, in terms of visual appeal, higher berms are better.

It takes one to three years for a newly planted succulent garden to fill in; by five years, it looks so good that people assume it has been there twenty.

OPPOSITE In Amy Gould's Bellingham, Washington, front yard, boulders provide an ideal microclimate for burgundy-leaved sedums, *Yucca elephantipes* (back left), *Dasylirion wheeleri*, and *Agave americana* 'Mediopicta Alba' (front center).

BELOW Berms elevate plants for better viewing and increase the plantable area. Succulents shown here include *Aeonium* 'Sunburst' (foreground), *Aloe vanbalenii* in bloom, *Portulacaria afra* 'Variegata', golden barrel cacti, and blue *Pilosocereus pachycladus*.

Queen palms give this garden a tropical ambience. Multiple *Agave attenuata* rosettes and drifts of blue *Senecio serpens* contrast in texture and color with a variegated ornamental grass (right). The grass in turn repeats the shape of the palm fronds and visually ties the upper and lower parts of the composition. The agaves are in scale with the setting, and a collection of smaller, colorful succulents are situated where they will be noticed—along the stairs.

When in drought

A lawn requires more water per square foot than anything else you might grow in the same space. It's a good play surface for pets and children, but for most activities, 500 to 800 square feet is plenty. In general, a garden of succulents and comparably waterwise ornamentals needs one-third to two-thirds less water than the same area of lawn.

It may seem daunting to remove and replace a lawn that has flanked your house for years, but think of it as a liberation. Your new succulent garden will free you from the need to mow and tend turf and the guilt of pouring water on it, and will reward you with the satisfaction of having an easy-care yard that's as sensible as it is beautiful.

Lawns can be eliminated by solarizing with clear plastic sheeting, thereby steaming the roots; by smothering with cardboard or sheets of newspaper piled with mulch; or by digging and disposing. All methods have pros and cons. Certain types of grass actually like being chopped up; it helps them spread. Solarizing not only kills grass, it also cooks beneficial soil organisms. Smothering can take months and is hit-or-miss. Treating turf with

a root-killing herbicide may be tempting because it's easy, but opponents say any chemical used on plants may have a long-lasting negative impact on the environment and anyone who comes into contact with it.

If you want some lawn but not a lot, take a bite out of your existing one. Reduced-size lawns tend to be more visually appealing if curved and serpentine rather than rectangular or square. Ornamental hardscape is another option. It requires no maintenance other than sweeping; creates a flat surface for parties, children's play, and ball-chasing dogs; and when done correctly adds beauty and character to the overall garden.

BELOW, LEFT Lovely vignettes such as this one in Los Angeles are, unfortunately, ephemeral. Blooms soon need deadheading; perennials, pruning; and grass, mowing. Ornamental shrubs will die without biweekly irrigation, except for the focal point— *Agave americana* 'Marginata', a tough Southwest succulent that just wants to be left alone.

BELOW, RIGHT Quartzite pavers enhance the yard while reducing the size of the lawn. The curved hardscape area serves as a demarcation between lawn and succulent bed, and the stones repeat hues found in the plants.

Eighteen months after its redo, the Gleason front yard has filled in. Plants need far less water and maintenance than the previous lawn and shrubs. Ornamental rocks include hefty boulders, fist-size stones, and small pebbles. The driveway is new, too. "Hardscape," says designer Steve McDearmon, "is the new black."

With the help of a designer and a professional installer, Chris and John Gleason of Carmel Valley, a neighborhood of San Diego, tore out their lawn, removed an ornamental pear tree and hedge, added a new irrigation system, demolished and upgraded the hardscape, and brought in amended soil, boulders and rocks, and succulents that range from ground covers to trees. The result is a climate-appropriate landscape that's enjoyable to take care of and look at.

Bob and Jeanette Mustacich of Goleta, California, enhanced their home's privacy and living-room view by creating a 700-square-foot sloped succulent garden in

When Chris and John Gleason bought their home, its front yard was indistinguishable from others in their housing development.

Alongside the Gleasons' entry path, *Agave lophantha* 'Quadricolor' and its offsets contrast with ornamental boulders. Smaller rocks and gravel fill unplanted areas.

Succulents in the five-year-old garden are primarily aloes, including pink *Aloe capitata*, large *A. rupestris*, octopus-shaped *A. vanbalenii*, trunk-forming *A. vaombe*, and, in the back, *A. dichotoma*. A curved pathway leads into the garden and emphasizes the focal point: a silvery blue Bismarck palm (*Bismarckia nobilis*).

ABOVE About a third of the rock went into building hidden retaining walls along the back and two sides of the Mustacich garden; the rest was incorporated into the design. Notice the 2-foot walkway between retaining walls and fence.

RIGHT The couple designed the slope so it crests near the fence, which allows them to see as much of the garden as possible from inside the house.

Bordering a sidewalk in San Diego's Point Loma neighborhood is a succulent garden planted with aloes, variegated aeoniums, *Agave attenuata*, barrel cacti, and blue *Senecio mandraliscae*. Included are a dark green sago palm (top right) and copper-hued boulders.

This hell strip (area between sidewalk and street) in San Diego is planted entirely with *Aloe ×nobilis*. Commonly called noble aloes, the plants need little care other than deadheading faded flowers in June.

their front yard. To do so, they brought in 30 cubic yards of succulent soil and 20 tons of rock.

Curbside borders can be challenging to maintain, especially if they need mowing, weeding, frequent watering, and debris removal. Yet such areas are visible to passersby and can positively or negatively impact your home's curb appeal, so leaving them untended isn't an option. For a simple but harmonious composition, repeat plant material and arrange ground covers in broad strokes. This is one instance where you needn't worry about a plant being invasive; when surrounded by concrete, it has nowhere to go.

If you install large agaves or aloes, know their size at maturity, lest they eventually encroach on sidewalks, steps, or street. You might plant the area with tough small succulents, such as 6-to-8-inch-diameter *Aloe ×nobilis* or *A. brevifolia*, which will offset and eventually cover every inch. Due to their prickles, these plants discourage kids and dogs from treading on them. Yet the prickles of these and other aloes pose no more danger than small points of wax. A downside is that over time they may become so dense, a curbside colony can make it difficult for passengers to exit parked cars.

Terraces That Turn Hillsides into Gardens

Steep terrain is challenging to landscape, but it's fun to explore a garden that you ascend or descend into, especially when each switchback reveals something new. On one side of the path is greenery; on the other, the view.

Every slope is different, but the basic approach to landscaping a hillside is to build retaining walls to create terraces connected by pathways and steps. The higher the wall, the more soil needed to fill it, but the less steep and larger the new planting area will be. Terraced beds lend themselves to herb and vegetable gardens, and to cascading succulents such as graptopetalums and burro tail (*Sedum morganianum*), as well as floriferous companions like ivy geraniums.

Mortarless retaining walls have built-in drainage because moisture seeps between the stones, creating an environment for naturally cliff-dwelling sedums, echeverias, dudleyas, and sempervivums.

Make sure any retaining wall can withstand pressure exerted on it by the slope it holds back. During construction, to enhance stability, dig a trench about a foot deep to hold the first course of stone. Angle the wall so

Rock walls retain the soil of a steep slope in Montecito, California. The bold forms of aloes, dasylirions, and blue agaves (*Agave franzosinii* and *A. ovatifolia*) contrast with finer-leaved shrubs.

that it inclines back slightly into the slope, 2 inches for every foot of height. If a great deal of earth has to be moved or retained, you may need a building permit and possibly a structural engineer.

When landscaping an erosion-prone slope, arrange plants in staggered rows. Build basins on each plant's downhill side using soil from the planting hole. Water with drip irrigation to minimize runoff. To hold the soil until the plants are established, blanket the area with jute netting, sold by the roll at home and garden centers; it will gradually decompose. Or use horizontal bands of straw wattle secured with metal stakes. Conceal the jute or straw with an organic mulch, which also helps water retention and if at least 6 inches deep is more effective than herbicides for weed control.

Succulent ground covers commonly called ice plants are popular because they spread readily and bloom spectacularly. Although such plants lessen the impact of rainwater on the soil and help decrease runoff, their roots are too shallow to stabilize a steep slope. It's best to combine them with deeper-rooted shrubs and trees.

OPPOSITE Terraces surrounding a hillside home in Austin, Texas, create planting beds for aloes, agaves, dasylirions, and more. The tan-colored topdressing is integral to the design.

Your Garden, from Dream to Reality

During your garden's planning stages, sketch its layout to scale on graph paper. If it's especially complex, a design software program can help. Include anything that won't change, such as the footprint of your house, property boundaries, walls, fences, driveway, mailbox, and where visitors park and open car doors.

Make several copies of the basic sketch and then use each to conceptualize a different garden plan. One might have straight pathways aligned on a central axis, perhaps with a succulent-planted fountain in the middle; another, paths that flow around peninsular beds. Keep in mind practical considerations such as utilities, tool storage, and a fenced area for dogs. Include walkways that lead to and connect outdoor areas for sitting, sunning, dining, and other activities tailored to your family's needs and recreational interests.

Next, plan the layout of each garden room, defining where various elements—such as large rocks, decking, outdoor furnishings, and container groupings—will go. You'll likely want to bring in amended soil that drains well, so position mounds of soil and boulders according to the highs and lows of the house. Represent trees as circles that approximate their size at maturity and use colored pencils to block in massed plantings. For a natural look, show ground-cover succulents in drifts. Keep in mind that in their native habitats, plants grow where rainwater flows.

Where to plant trees and what kinds are important choices. Once established, a tree can't be moved—or removed—without expense and inconvenience, so before you install one, find out how large it will grow, how much leaf litter it will shed, and whether it's prone to disease. Also know the tree's water requirements. A tropical tree in a succulent bed, for example, may suffer from too little irrigation. Depending on where a tree is positioned, it can shade a sunny window or sitting area; reduce glare from a swimming pool, windows, white walls, or pavement; and deflect (or redirect) wind. If you want shade in summer and sun in winter, plant deciduous trees.

Another important choice is whether to install an in-ground, automatic irrigation system—a great convenience in hot, dry climates. Such systems (which can also be used manually) can be programmed according to zone, so that a lawn receives more water than,

Landscape designer Linda Bresler drew a sketch to scale of the proposed garden of client Elisabeth Matthys in Poway, California. The drawing shows planting beds, pathways, an outdoor sitting area that overlooks the view, and the existing trees they decided to keep.

say, a bank of ice plants. Minimize water waste with micro-sprayers, bubblers, low-angle nozzles, and drip irrigation. Spray heads provide options in terms of how much area they cover and the volume of water they project. Drip puts water where a plant needs it and prevents overspray that wastes water and promotes weed growth.

Hire a professional for tasks beyond your expertise, such as building berms, terraces, and retaining walls; tackling drainage and other grading concerns; or installing pathways, irrigation systems, outdoor lighting, pergolas, decks, patios, or water features. Most landscape designers charge an hourly fee and can provide an estimate on an entire project, from initial plans to installation.

If you see a garden in your area that you like, ask the owners who helped create and/or install it, and if they'd recommend that person. Also check with horticultural societies, garden clubs, the local Cactus and Succulent Society of America (CSSA) chapter, and nurseries that specialize in dry-climate plants. If a community college in your area has a landscape design program, you might offer your garden as a class project. Organizations such as the American Society of Landscape Architects (ASLA) and, in California, the California Landscape Contractors Association (CLCA) can provide names of members in your area. Request to see past projects—not just photos, but actual gardens you can visit. Rapport is important; make sure the landscaper shares your aesthetic, welcomes your input, and is an expert on the growth habits and cultivation requirements of in-ground succulents and low-water companion plants.

The Matthys garden, two years after installation, has become a three-dimensional representation of the designer's sketch.

Specialty Gardens That Showcase Succulents

More than any other type of plant, succulents lend themselves to imaginative, nontraditional gardens that illustrate their owner's style, imagination, and personality. Because of their classic and unusual shapes, unlimited foliage colors, and ease of maintenance, succulent gardens and vignettes can range from practical to whimsical and might even combine the two.

In this chapter, you'll discover that regardless of where you live—whether seashore, desert, or chilly Northeast—succulents are eager to accommodate you, in the ground, in containers, or even on your roof. Southwesterners have the option of using cacti, yuccas, and agaves as living fences that provide a low-water green backdrop, security barricade, and wildfire barrier. And if it seems your property is nothing but a rock pile, consider yourself fortunate—garden designers view boulders as a bonus, and succulents thrive in rocky terrain and crevices.

If you find a certain type of succulent fascinating, by all means create a garden with your collection in mind. I'll also intrigue you with succulent-scapes that resemble coral reefs, gardens that suggest tapestries, and in-ground vignettes designed to whisk you to fantasy worlds.

FEATURED GARDEN

Hannah Jarson's aloe Eden

Large aloes are the stars of the 2-acre garden surrounding the contemporary home in Rancho Santa Fe, California, that Hannah Jarson shares with husband, Howard. Aloe bloom spires, which range from pale shades of yellow through vivid orange and crimson, harmonize in an orchestra of color. The crescendo happens late winter through spring, but one or more species of aloe is in bloom year-round.

Landscape designer Tom Jesch of Waterwise Botanicals nursery designed the layout of a succulent garden that Hannah has been enhancing ever since. The soil is clay, rocky, and sandy, so before planting it's amended to provide a friable mix of one-third native soil, one-third compost, and one-third pumice. Irrigation is via overhead sprinklers. "We used to have drip, but it isn't feasible when you have thousands of plants," Howard says. "We were constantly checking to make sure emitters weren't plugged." Hannah adds, "Overhead watering isn't as economical as drip, but then, we don't water much"—on average, once a week during hot, dry weather and not at all in winter if rainfall is adequate.

Aloes can be tricky to identify, for a couple of reasons. First, they hybridize readily, giving rise to plants that straddle the boundaries between the species. Second, some species are quite variable in themselves, with different forms having varying appearances and flower colors. But to Hannah it's not about names as much as personalities. "I anthropomorphize my succulents," she admits with a smile. "I congratulate them when they bloom or recover from some mishap." "Hannah celebrates the birth of new plants and mourns those that die," attests Howard.

Howard has discovered an unexpected benefit of growing aloes: they attract nectar-loving birds. It's an unforgettable experience, he says, "when a hummingbird hovers in front of you and looks you right in the eye."

Aloe 'Hercules' dominates a bed that includes *A. rubroviolacea* in bloom and several species of agaves. The topdressing is decomposed granite.

In keeping with Hannah's love of color, this *Aloe capitata* hybrid has bicolored flowers, and its leaves range from teal blue through shades of lavender, rose red, and orange. *Aloe speciosa* in the background also offers bicolored (red-and-cream) blooms.

ABOVE Hannah has both the red- and orange-flowering varieties of *Aloe cameronii*, which she prizes for its sun-reddened crimson leaves. Enhancing the front yard are *Agave* 'Blue Glow', *Agave parryi* var. *truncata*, a red-flowering *Euphorbia milii*, *Portulacaria afra* 'Variegata', and golden barrel cacti.

LEFT Airy *Aloe vanbalenii* bloom spires contrast with the home's rectilinear presence. At lower right, not in flower, is a colony of *A. distans*.

TOP *Aloe dorotheae* and *Senecio vitalis* are among succulents thriving on a rocky ledge in Honolulu, Hawaii. Roots readily penetrate coarse volcanic soil that offers the added benefit of draining rapidly.

BOTTOM Bright green *Echeveria pallida* (in bloom) grows atop a pile of rounded river rocks. Nestled amid the rocks is blue *Echeveria imbricata*, and in the background is a cluster of *Agave mitis* var. *albidior* (formerly *A. celsii* var. *albicans*).

Boulder and Rock Gardens

From a design standpoint, a garden can never have too many rocks. Boulders, crushed rock, cobbles, and pebbles lend interest to the terrain, add texture, create focal points and vignettes, and cover bare dirt so the landscape has a finished look. Flat rocks can serve as benches when positioned alongside pathways or patios. If you're fortunate, your property already has some you can use. If not, rock suppliers offer everything from pea gravel sold by the sack to behemoths that have to be lowered into place with a crane.

Many beautiful types of decorative rock are available, including Arizona sandstones with cream-and-orange swirls. There's nothing wrong with using rocks that make a statement, provided that's what you're aiming for; otherwise, they may look unnatural. A better choice might be rocks and boulders found in your area that blend with your terrain. Stones sometimes incorporate colorful veins and silvery patches that can be echoed by similarly colored succulents. But do avoid creating a pancake-flat yard populated by lonely looking cacti spaced equidistantly in a sea of white gravel—unless, of course, you *want* a retirement-community cliché from the sixties.

If you're bringing in large rocks to enhance your front yard but are uncertain where to place them, look at your home in terms of mass and aim to balance it. For example, if the house has a gable or porch on the right as viewed from the street, situate the largest boulder on the left. As though painting a landscape, position the biggest rock first, then continue with progressively smaller ones. Partially bury large rocks so they look like they've

Designer Michael Buckner pays as much attention to rocks and boulders as he does to the succulents he specializes in. For this sloping garden, he turned cobbles on their sides to suggest a torrent, handpicked boulders for their shapes and colors, and even persuaded his client to paint the wall gold to provide a perfect backdrop.

Assorted colorful and collectible rocks in this Sierrascape suggest the backcountry. Designer Gary Bartl positioned flagstone pieces upright to resemble mountain peaks and hold soil away from the wall. Succulents of all sorts populate the display, located near the home's entry. When seen from inside, framed by a window, it serves as a focal point.

Because it grows along the cliffs of the artists' community of Laguna Beach, California, *Aloe arborescens* has been immortalized in numerous paintings. At lower left is *Agave attenuata*.

been there forever. A common mistake, especially when adding a boulder to a slope, is to let the underside show. Even though you know it's stable, it won't appear to be and will strike others as unsettling.

Most succulents thrive in rock gardens. As in the plants' native habitats, stones elevate and support their crowns, prevent water from pooling around them, keep mud and debris off their leaves, and moderate temperatures. Soil in pockets between boulders tends to stay warm and moist, which promotes rapid root formation. And when rosette succulents cluster amid and around boulders, they have a charming, settled-in look.

TOP A larger-than-life seahorse makes other aspects of this vignette appear smaller in comparison, including *Diso-cactus flagelliformis* (at top) and *Echeveria agavoides* (foreground).

BOTTOM Aloes and aeoniums thrive in a Carmel, California, seaside garden, as does *Senecio mandraliscae*, which mirrors the blue of sky and water.

Seaside and Sea-Theme Gardens

Although a mild maritime climate is ideal for the majority of succulents, growing them within reach of salt spray can be problematic, as it is for most plants. A garden mere steps from the waves is exposed to wind, salt, and dampness much more than if it were on the opposite side of the house.

Evaluate which area of your ocean-facing garden gets the strongest winds and plant accordingly. If they won't block your view, agaves, aloes, yuccas, and paddle cacti look good silhouetted against sea and sky. Use large specimens as windbreaks and plant smaller succulents—such as aeoniums and dudleyas—in their lee.

Living near the ocean may prompt you to create a sea-theme succulent garden, but you can also adopt this motif if you're landlocked. Much of the fun is viewing the plants in fresh ways. Succulents you previously took for granted or hadn't noticed may strike you as having tide pool potential.

Give your undersea scene elevations and canyons so when you look at it, you get a sense that you're snorkeling past it. Fill crevices with potting soil and tuck small succulents or cuttings into them. Top-dress with crushed lava rock, fine pea gravel, and sand strewn with bits of blue and green tumbled glass. Props are important and might include a rusty anchor, a hefty chain, or a half-buried urn (perhaps planted with a rat-tail cactus that suggests a moray eel).

Cacti and succulents that are *crested*—a term that refers to a tendency to form tight, convoluted shapes—are desirable in a succulent seascape because they resemble coral. You might also fill seashells with potting soil and insert small plants that resemble sea creatures.

ABOVE Variegated *Agave gypsophila*,
Crassula capitella 'Campfire', and a metal
sea star resemble reef inhabitants.

RIGHT Designer Steve Sutherland of Santa
Cruz, California, used *Cotyledon orbiculata* as foam for the crest of this breaking
wave, and red echeverias to suggest algae
swept up in the flow.

Marine life look-alikes

The best succulents for an undersea-theme garden are those that lack characteristics of terrestrial plants: woody stems, a treelike structure, and leafy foliage. Generally, rosette succulents that look like daisies (such as most aeoniums) don't fit the fantasy.

Coral (branching) *Crassula ovata* cultivars, *Euphorbia tirucalli* 'Sticks on Fire'

Coral (knobby) crested and monstrose specimens, *Faucaria tigrina*, fenestrarias

Coral (overlapping) *Kalanchoe luciae*

Eel grass *Euphorbia leucodendron, Pedilanthus macrocarpus, Senecio anteuphorbium, S. mandraliscae*

Jellyfish tentacles *Disocactus flagelliformis*, medusoid euphorbias

Kelp *Alluaudia procera, Sansevieria trifasciata*

Octopuses *Agave gypsophila, A. vilmoriniana, Aloe vanbalenii*

Sea anemones *Euphorbia caput-medusae, E. flanaganii*

Sea snakes *Crassula* 'Baby's Necklace', *Disocactus martianus, Cleistocactus icosagonus*

Sea stars small agaves, dwarf aloes, *Dyckia* 'Brittle Star', *Haworthia attenuata*

Sea urchins *Euphorbia horrida, E. polygona*

Sponge colony *Crassula ovata* 'Gollum' (massed cuttings), *Euphorbia obesa* (clustered)

Though indigenous to northern Peru and southern Ecuador, *Cleistocactus icosagonus* appears to come from somewhere deep in the sea.

At aptly named Desert Theater Nursery in Escondido, California, late afternoon sun makes cactus spines glow.

OPPOSITE Gardens in Arizona are often landscaped with native succulents such as agaves, yuccas, and prickly pears, all of which thrive beyond the region. Rising above the roofline of this Tucson home is an ocotillo, and in the foreground is black-foot daisy, a summer-blooming perennial.

Desert Gardens with Style

Desert and cactus gardens have an austere, unfussy aesthetic that for some people represents the ultimate in refined elegance. The appeal may have to do with how sunlight illuminates spines, creating halos; how the plants' simple outlines are restful to the eye; or that such edgy, keep-away plants—like feral cats—can be rewarding to tame.

The first edition of *Designing with Succulents* shows a residential succulent and cactus garden owned by Chris and Margaret Sullivan in San Diego's Kensington neighborhood. The couple sold the house several years later, and because the new owners planned to tear out the garden, the Sullivans salvaged many of its finest specimens. Their new garden, also in San Diego, has since been featured in *Sunset* magazine as an example of how good-looking a no-water, no-maintenance garden can be.

The Palm Springs–style garden the Sullivans created for their new front yard needs no water other than the occasional rainstorm, although they do hose off the barrel cacti in summer if dusty. Enhancing the composition are boulders from the couple's previous garden, and clusters of golden barrel cacti in randomly spaced groupings.

Because the soil was compacted "like concrete," Chris says, and drained poorly, they had it removed to a depth of several feet and brought in 10 yards of decomposed granite for the substrate. On top of that went a

RIGHT, TOP Chris and Margaret Sullivan's previous garden, as shown in the first edition of *Designing with Succulents*, was five years old at the time. The garden included cacti that had been mature when planted, such as the large trichocereus at far right. Soil is two-thirds decomposed granite and one-third cactus mix, top-dressed with golden crushed rock.

RIGHT, BOTTOM The contemporary style of the Sullivans' new home makes a good backdrop for their minimalistic garden. They chose the greenish tan house color to go well with columnar cacti and *Yucca rostrata* trees. Topdressing, like that of their earlier garden, is gravel the color of desert sand.

Columnar cacti dominate a rock garden at Lone Pine Gardens, a succulent nursery in northern California. Along with the ceroids are succulent ice plants, cotyledons, sedums, and bulbine.

At Ronald McKitrick's Hillside Desert Botanical Gardens in Yakima, Washington, a yucca, scarlet hedgehog cactus (*Echinocereus coccineus*), and *Lewisia cotyledon* provide cold-hardy color and texture.

The succulent garden at Kapi'olani Community College in Honolulu, Hawaii, incorporates numerous happy cacti, despite a tropical climate with 25 inches average annual precipitation. Along with the cacti are a trio of fat-trunked *Pachypodium lamerei* with leafy topknots.

blend of DG and cactus mix, top-dressed (after plants were installed) with a warm-hued crushed rock. Chris uses long-handled tweezers to extract weeds close to the cacti and applies no pesticides or fertilizer. Although they live in a canyon and neighbors complain about rabbits, the critters have shown no interest in the Sullivan garden. Its installation probably cost a little more up front than a typical front yard landscape, Chris says, "but it's a hundred times less work than a lawn."

Cacti are among the world's most resilient and adaptable plants. All they ask is that their roots don't sit in water, they get half a day of sunshine or more, and they have adequate air circulation so pests don't settle. If you select climate-appropriate varieties, it's possible to have a beautiful in-ground garden of collectible cacti well beyond the desert Southwest.

In Ronald McKitrick's half-acre Hillside Desert Botanical Gardens in Yakima, Washington, cacti blast into bloom in colors so bright they're barely to be believed. The low desert garden is in the rain shadow of the Cascade Range. McKitrick has spent more than thirty years experimenting with succulents to see which will survive Yakima's dry inland climate of 6 inches of rainfall a year, summer highs in the 90s F, and wintertime lows of 0°F or below. Due to the proximity of volcanoes, pumice is readily available as a soil amendment. In addition to growing agaves, sempervivums, sedums, yuccas, and more, McKitrick, known for using a shop vacuum to clean leaf debris from chollas, grows three hundred varieties of cactus, most of which he started from seed.

At the Western Colorado Botanical Gardens in Grand Junction, *Opuntia basilaris* is just coming into bloom. Alongside it is a white-spined cholla, *Sedum rupestre* 'Blue Spruce', and with dime-size pale pink flowers, *Delosperma* 'Kelaidis'.

Centers of rosettes in the collapsed stand of *Aloe arborescens* (center, right) in Suzy Schaefer's garden are still green and viable, despite heat estimated to have exceeded 1,000°F.

Behind the wall are the remains of a house lost to wildfire in 2007. Three specimens of *Agave americana* along the wall appear relatively unscathed—including the one at right beneath a piece of charred wood.

Firewise Gardens

Late summer and autumn are wildfire season in southern California. Native chaparral is dry after no rainfall for six months or more, and hot, dry Santa Ana winds blow from the east along canyons leading to the sea. Homeowners who live in rural areas—as my husband and I do—are as alert as meerkats, watching for plumes of smoke on the horizon and sniffing the air for any hint of smoke. Jeff and I and our two dogs were evacuated during the wildfires of 2007, but thankfully the danger came no closer than 11 miles. When we returned, everything was intact, but our home's entry resembled an ashtray, and the garden's hardscape was black with soot.

That same day I received an email message from Suzy Schaefer, owner of the garden on the cover of the first edition of *Designing with Succulents*, which had been released six months earlier. The subject line was "Succulents saved our home." Santa Ana winds had sent the Witch Creek Fire through a canyon bordering the Schaefer property, burning a house across the street to the ground. The fire turned palm trees in the canyon into blackened silhouettes and scorched the base of a eucalyptus tree a few feet from Suzy's art studio—the part of the house closest to the canyon. She credited succulent ground covers, jade plants, and a 5-foot-tall stand of *Aloe arborescens* with serving as a fire barrier. When I

visited soon afterward, the aloe's scorched leaves were collapsed and the color of putty, but surprisingly, the center of each rosette was green. Later, Suzy was able to salvage enough of the aloe to take cuttings and restart it.

In the ensuing week, local TV news sent a camera crew to the Schaefer garden and interviewed both of us on the topic of succulents as firebreak plants. The story was picked up by the Associated Press, and I wrote about it for the *Los Angeles Times*. My favorite quote in the article is from Gary Lyons, curator of the desert collection at the Huntington Botanical Gardens in San Marino, California, who noted that agaves, aloes, and opuntias don't burn or transmit fire but rather cook. "I wondered why there was no code requirement or law that requires developers and residents to use succulents in high fire areas," he said. "Why should taxpayers shoulder the firefighting costs of a hillside development's incendiary landscape?"

Indeed, if you live in a wildfire-prone region, a garden of juicy leaved plants can be one more weapon in your arsenal of protection. Although succulents typically are more fire resistant than other kinds of plants, a notable exception is *Carpobrotus edulis* (pickleweed, Hottentot fig); if dry leaves beneath the ground cover's fingerlike foliage catch fire, they can smolder unseen even after the blaze is extinguished, creating a hazard for homeowners and firefighters alike.

Why succulents are fire resistant

Fire-prevention experts advise homeowners to plant succulents because they meet these criteria:

- Plant tissues have a high moisture content.

- Leaves don't contain flammable oils or other volatile chemicals.

- Many varieties grow close to the ground, but even the largest won't provide a fire ladder that enables flames to reach the eaves of a structure.

- Plants thrive in dry, sunny areas (typical of fire-prone sites).

- Succulents stay green and healthy with minimal irrigation, so they are suited to perimeter areas likely to receive less water than those closer to the structure.

This security fence of paddle cacti, chollas, and *Agave angustifolia* planted along a property line also serves as a wildfire barrier.

Atop their garden's chicken coop, Rebecca and Jeff Nickols of Strafford, Missouri, installed a green roof planted with stonecrops. The couple based the design on the sedum-topped birdhouses they make and sell seasonally at Farmers Market of the Ozarks and on Etsy.

A green roof at Emory Knoll Farms in Maryland includes a variety of stonecrops (sedums) chosen for their contrasting colors and shapes. Serpentine drifts appear to flow.

Succulents in the Sky: Green Roof Gardens

Another way to use succulents as fire-retardant plants is to grow them on rooftops. Succulents can make a roof an "extinguisher" of sorts. A green roof can also provide an appealing patchwork of plants and give you more space in which to garden.

Besides retarding fire, green roofs atop homes or on outbuildings such as sheds and carports can absorb storm water, keep the building cooler in summer, and serve as habitat for birds and beneficial insects such as butterflies and bees. Succulents—sedums in particular—are among the most popular green roof plants because they're tough, shallow rooted, and compact, and require minimal water. Roots of green roof plants knit together in a thin layer of soil watered by rain or, in dry climates, by drip irrigation or micro sprayers. (A typical green roof requires a minimum of 25 to 30 inches of rainfall per year.) All green roofs need regular water while the plants are becoming established, but the goal is a self-sustaining ecosystem appropriate to both climate and region.

Ideally, plants atop a roof reseed or offset and need only occasional pruning, deadheading, and replanting. To enhance floral color and add textural interest, annuals and accent plants can be interspersed with succulents. Shallow-rooted herbaceous perennials such as yarrow, dianthus, phlox, campanula, germander, viola, and oregano are easily incorporated, depending on the location and exposure. Annuals sown as seeds can add quick color and cover bare patches, thereby defeating weeds. Bulbs such as crocus and grape hyacinth are useful for adding pops of color in early spring.

Phoenix landscape architect Steve Martino installed a shallow planter atop a shed, filled it with soil and decomposed granite, and shingled it with cactus pads. "It's my take on thatch," he says. "I thought the shed would collapse from the weight, but it's lasted six years." The pads haven't grown much because their roots have no place to go. Like goldfish, "they knew their confined conditions and just stopped growing," Martino says. They also survived a fire that destroyed an adjacent carport. About half the pads were scorched, but they recovered after a few years. The roof, which bakes in the desert sun, is infrequently watered with micro sprayers.

To create a green roof, a waterproofing membrane is first applied to protect the building from moisture and root penetration; then a layer of growing medium; and last, plants suited to the climate and conditions. Surprisingly, a properly installed green roof will last longer than its traditional counterpart (on average, thirty years). Such longevity is attributed to the fact that plants and substrate prevent solar rays from damaging the waterproof membrane. A green roof's protective layers also shield the structure from wind, water, and ice. Newer systems take advantage of technologically advanced materials and are thinner, more lightweight, and easier to install.

If you're considering a green roof, make sure the building can support the weight, which is much greater than that of a conventional roof, and that the slope and drainage are within acceptable limits. Check your local building codes and consult an experienced contractor or structural engineer. Also consider how much maintenance it's likely to require.

BELOW Inspired by gardens and structures at Findhorn in Scotland, Pennsylvania landscape architect Margot Taylor installed a straw-bale hut in her Kennett Square garden. Its green roof is planted with *Delosperma nubigenum* and a half-dozen sedums (including *Sedum sexangulare*, *S. album*, and *S. rupestre* 'Angelina').

BOTTOM Cactus pads that form a green roof atop a shed in Phoenix, Arizona, were originally laid flat like shingles. Over time they turned upward.

Cold-Climate Succulent Gardens

In midwinter at Plant Delights Nursery in Raleigh, North Carolina, snow outlines *Agave salmiana* cultivars.

If you appreciate the geometric forms of succulents and their minimal water requirements but live in a climate where winters are too cold and rainy for frost-tender, rot-prone varieties, grow sempervivums (hens and chicks), sedums (stonecrops), lewisias, and orostachys. Several kinds of aloes, agaves, yuccas, ice plants, and cacti will likely thrive in your garden, too. A nice bonus is they look great dusted with snow, which also insulates the plants, protecting them from colder temperatures.

Among the larger succulents that tolerate temperatures to 5°F and below are *Agave havardiana*, *A. lechuguilla*, *A. neomexicana*, *A. parryi*, *A. salmiana*, *A. toumeyana*, and *A. utahensis*; and *Yucca filamentosa*, *Y. flaccida*, *Y. glauca*, *Y. gloriosa*, *Y. harrimaniae*, and *Y. schottii*. Midsize *Aloe striatula* and *A. polyphylla* also thrive in temperatures well below freezing.

Sedum rupestre 'Angelina', burgundy sempervivums, and *Sedum* 'Soft Cloud' create cold-hardy carpets of color in a Spring Grove, Illinois, garden.

More than fifty types of *Opuntia* and a dozen varieties of *Echinocereus* will grow where temperatures drop below 0°F, according to members of the Ottawa Cactus Club, who have grown and tested them in their gardens.

Widely cultivated *Sedum* (stonecrop) species that are cold tolerant and will grow in most zones include ground covers *S. acre* (goldmoss sedum), *S. album*, *S. anglicum*, *S. rupestre* 'Angelina' (Angelina stonecrop), and *S. spurium*. Numerous shrublike sedums that grow to about 18 inches tall and die to the ground in winter and that are prized for their long-stemmed flower clusters are also hardy. *Sempervivum* (hens and chicks or houseleek) is perhaps the best-known genus of frost-tolerant succulents. Semps will tolerate temperatures down to −30°F but are at risk during summer heat spells in excess of 80°F.

Delosperma cooperi, an ice plant that produces magenta flowers and makes an excellent ground cover, is hardy to −20°F. A yellow-blooming variety reputed to be even more cold tolerant is *D. nubigenum*. Lewisias (to −40°F), along with orostachys (to −32°F), are wonderful small succulents for containers and rock gardens.

In regions that receive more than 20 inches of rainfall annually, grow succulents in berms that are 70 to 80 percent fine gravel or crushed lava rock, with the rest potting soil and coarse sand. Keep in mind that boulders and stone walls absorb the sun's heat and radiate it at night, thereby creating a microclimate several degrees warmer than the rest of the garden.

In a Georgetown, Colorado, rock garden at 8,500 feet (zone 5a), hardy sedums steal the show in summer, blooming in rosy tones that echo those of the home.

In a British Columbia garden, stonecrops (sedums) and hens and chicks (sempervivums) have found ideal growing conditions amid rocks surrounding a pond.

Red-tipped green *Sempervivum tectorum* and other species of hens and chicks grow in moss-covered troughs in Marietta and Ernie O'Byrne's Eugene, Oregon, garden.

At the Chanticleer public garden in Pennsylvania, a gravel pathway is flanked by *Delosperma cooperi*.

Peeling paint on the mullions of a window from an architectural salvage shop makes a textural backdrop for an assortment of floral-style succulent arrangements in Campo de' Fiori pots. Use of the same material—aged terra-cotta—gives the grouping continuity and sophistication, while the pots' varying shapes, sizes, and heights lend contrast.

Creative Container Gardens

You don't need grounds to have a gorgeous succulent garden. The plants can be potted and grouped on patios, balconies, and decks—anyplace that receives adequate light and air circulation. And because pots can be moved and sheltered, they make it possible to cultivate succulents that might not thrive in the harsher environment of your yard. If you lack space, grow the plants in vertical gardens and hanging-orb terrariums.

Unlike potted annuals, which need to be replaced seasonally, and perennials that need repotting after a year or two, succulents tend to last several years in containers. Keep basic design principles in mind as you pair plants with pots, compose arrangements, and decide where a container garden should go. Pots 6 inches in diameter or smaller are fine for intimate sitting areas, but you'll need larger containers to make a statement in your garden. Make groupings dynamic by using pots that share one or more design elements, such as material, color, shape, and/or glaze.

Think outside the pot. Window boxes, urns, shells, and even repurposed auto parts can serve as containers that display succulents in creative and intriguing ways. Moreover, because many succulents can survive for extended periods by living off their stored reserves, cuttings can be glued onto items that range from license plate frames to holiday ornaments. To give the plants a moisture-holding medium to root into, first glue a layer of sphagnum moss

RIGHT An asymmetrical arrangement in a 6-inch pot with a metallic sheen features two outstanding succulents for containers: golden *Kalanchoe tomentosa* 'Chocolate Soldier' (left) and wavy leaved *Echeveria* 'Neon Breakers'.

A diminutive garden in a glass orb includes *Echeveria* 'Lola' and *E. agavoides* rosettes.

onto the object, then glue the cuttings to the moss. (Use a low-temperature glue gun or waterproof craft glue.)

Containers can transform a soilless (and soulless) urban balcony into an inviting, easy-care garden space. Being the closest thing to plastic in the plant kingdom has its advantages. Succulents need little pruning or deadheading, grow slowly when their roots are confined, and come in varieties suited to any container and amount of sun or lack thereof. And where no hose is handy, plants with minimal water needs are ideal, especially when drainage is problematic.

Succulents lend themselves to vertical gardens (living walls) because the plants are shallow rooted, stay compact, survive even if the growing medium dries out, and come in colors useful for creating patterns and designs. Options range from small framed "living pictures" in soil-filled boxes to entire wall systems complete with irrigation and drainage. Regardless of size or complexity, all enable their owners to enjoy and tend a garden in minimal horizontal space.

An automotive air filter from the sixties presents a riff on wreaths.

BELOW For my online Craftsy class, I hot-glued sphagnum moss to the lower right quarter of a grapevine wreath, then glued kalanchoe cuttings and echeveria rosettes to the moss. Floral wire also helps secure them, lest their weight pull them loose. Until they outgrew the arrangement about a year later, the plants needed only occasional pinching back and a weekly spritzing to hydrate their whiskery roots.

ABOVE Durable, soil-filled fabric pockets conceal a concrete block wall and create a vertical garden at eye level for anyone using the spa. The wall's 110 succulents and bromeliads, planted at the time of installation, filled in within six months.

BELOW *Haworthia attenuata* rosettes populate a shell atop a rustic table with wood grain that resembles wet beach sand.

ABOVE This 112-square-foot living wall in Encinitas, California, is unusual in that it's on a radius. Colorful succulents in the abstract design include orange coppertone stonecrop, yellow-and-green *Aeonium* 'Kiwi', blue *Senecio serpens*, and burgundy *Aeonium* 'Zwartkop'.

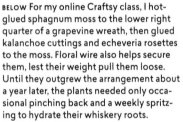

A balcony in downtown San Francisco has a clean-lined, contemporary look well suited to sleek, sculptural succulents. *Aloe barberae* trees fill vertical spaces and a crested myrtillocactus serves as both conversation piece and focal point. Yellow margins of sansevieria leaves repeat the color of outdoor furniture, as do barrel cacti in spherical pots.

Peter Bailey's barrel cactus checkerboard looks good year-round and is virtually maintenance free.

Santa Barbara designer Pat Brodie installed two 18-by-20-foot geometric gardens side by side so that they'd look square when seen from the home higher on the hill. The boxwoodlike plant is *Myrsine africana*, and the cross hedge *Teucreum chamaedrys*. Succulents in the rectangles are *Aloe greenii*, silver *Dudleya brittonii*, a cultivar of *Aeonium decorum*, *Crassula arborescens* subsp. *undulatifolia*, and *Echeveria agavoides*. On the slope in the foreground grow *Agave ovatifolia*, dasylirions, and aloes.

Geometric and Tapestry Gardens

Succulents with colorful leaves, compact shapes, and a tidy growth habit are perfect for patterned and tapestry gardens. Such geometric or abstract plantings are fun to create and offer opportunities to display succulents in novel and appealing ways.

Southern California homeowner Peter Bailey created a checkerboard of golden barrel cacti in an area of his yard visible from upstairs windows. He first installed drip irrigation, then lined the 700-square-foot area with black plastic to prevent weeds. After positioning twenty-five concrete pavers 2 feet apart to create a grid, he cut into the plastic and planted the cacti in the intersections, and then top-dressed exposed areas with crushed rock. To blend the area with the succulent garden beyond, he replaced one barrel cactus with a tree aloe.

For years, the focal point of my own garden was a rectangular bed of fifteen rose bushes planted in rows. It was pretty in spring, but in winter it became an 11-by-22-foot bed of naked, thorny branches sticking up at regular intervals—which, for much of the year, constituted the view from the living room windows.

Eventually I removed the rose bushes and turned the bed into a succulent tapestry. The succulents—many of which were cuttings—filled in within six months. For nearly a decade, the tapestry was lush and tidy, required minimal maintenance, and enhanced the view year-round. Best of all, this 240-square-foot area of the garden used two-thirds less water than required by the rose garden and produced showy, long-lasting flowers. Pathways of dymondia (a low-water, nonsucculent ground cover) enabled access to all areas of the tapestry, so I could weed, deadhead, and divide the succulents without stepping on them.

Nearby oak trees eventually grew to a point where the tapestry was too shaded—not good for the plants but perfect for a patio. Since it occupied the only level space in my yard, I paved the area with flagstone. Using existing plants and adding a few, San Diego designer Laura Eubanks installed two new succulent tapestries (about 200 square feet total) in adjacent sunny areas. Approximately half of each is top-dressed with rivers of crushed rock that enhance the design, enable access, and require even less upkeep than the plants.

My garden's original succulent tapestry had an agave in each corner and a potted dasylirion in the middle surrounded by aeoniums.

The larger of my garden's succulent tapestries includes rivers of red and black lava rock. The white criva (crushed rock that's coarser than sand but finer than gravel) was sprayed with a stabilizer that prevents it from blowing or washing away. A perennial vine, trained onto a wrought iron stand, is original to the area.

At each of this geometric garden's four corners is a slender *Dracaena marginata* tree in a spherical pot. In the beds are red-leaved *Aloe vaombe*, slender-leaved yuccas, green *Agave desmetiana*, and ornamental grasses.

Laura Eubanks tends her client's Hobbit garden and village. Round pebble pavers incorporated into the design enable a Gulliver-sized gardener to enter the village without squashing tiny plants and people.

Diminutive Landscapes

Like a bonsai collection, a small-scale landscape enables its owner to enjoy gardening in minimal outdoor space. Fairy gardens are one option, and numerous accessories for them are available, but do think beyond them. Aim for a miniature world that transports you to a separate place and time, perhaps even a different continent. Consider it a trip to an exotic destination that you orchestrate based on your preferences, interests, and imagination.

Must-dos for miniature gardens:

- Elevate the scene for better viewing and ease of maintenance, perhaps atop a terrace, on a slope, or in a raised bed. Locate it near a sitting area, where it will enhance a view or create a garden focal point, and will offer visitors a delightful discovery.

- Prepare the area as you would any bed for succulents. Remove weeds and plants likely to encroach, and add coarse, fast-draining soil. Sculpt the terrain to create hills and valleys, packing the soil firmly so it won't shift or settle. Incorporate a paving stone or flat area if the garden will be difficult to take care of without stepping into it.

- Choose a main viewing angle without a distracting background. Consider how the composition will look when framed by a camera lens. Decide on sight lines, focal points, and pathways that invite exploration. Partially conceal a few areas to lend a sense of mystery.

- Browse nurseries for tiny succulents and trade cuttings of the same with friends. Select small succulents that suggest much larger plants typical of the climate, region, and theme you're portraying. Group or arrange plants as they might grow in nature. Place bigger plants and buildings in the foreground, smaller but similar ones in the background to create an optical illusion that the garden is larger or longer than it actually is. Bury large rocks enough to anchor them and make them look well established.

- Ensure that potentially large succulents stay small. To dwarf a succulent, slide it out of its pot, root-ball and all, and line the pot with window screen or weed barrier cloth. (This keeps roots from taking hold in the surrounding soil yet allows drainage.) Before returning the plant to its pot, cut off the rim so it won't show. If need be, after burying the pot, prop the plant upright with rocks. This method also works well with pups and cuttings.

- Add a pebbled streambed dug below grade. Line the bed with sand and strew bits of

BELOW A branched cutting of *Kalanchoe tomentosa* 'Chocolate Soldier' (right) serves as a tree. In the upper terrace are sedum and aeonium rosettes, dark green *Crassula muscosa* (watch-chain crassula), bright yellow mounds of *Sedum rupestre* 'Lemon Coral', and dymondia.

crushed, tumbled glass to suggest sunlight sparkling on water. Embed a small mirror in a low-lying, level area to resemble a pond or lake. Top-dress with small stones and drifts of crushed rocks the size of peppercorns (criva).

• Keep the area free of pine needles and fallen leaves that might compromise the fantasy and the health of the plants. If your fingers are too large or glochids are a concern, groom plants with long, slender tweezers, scissors, or forceps.

• Consider how your mini-landscape could be further enhanced. For example, you might stencil or paint diminutive buildings with patterns that suggest tile. Tiny gardens, like their larger counterparts, continually need editing—which of course is much of the fun of having one.

Designer Laura Eubanks created a 30-foot-long, 6-foot-wide Hobbit village along the top of a retaining wall for a client who collects Cotswold-style cottages made of weatherproof resin. Eubanks repurposed roofing tiles found on the property as retaining walls that resemble cliffs. She chose succulents because they grow slowly and noninvasively and because the zone 9b garden bakes in hot afternoon sun. "You'd think succulents wouldn't look right in an English cottage garden," Eubanks says, "but the plants come in every shape, size, and texture." When a visitor asked Eubanks, "But don't Hobbits live underground?" she quipped, "Not in southern California they don't."

The main components of my own garden's miniature landscape, located alongside a flight of stone steps, are inexpensive terra-cotta buildings from an import store, flagstone remnants from a paving project, and an assortment of small cacti, crassulas, and euphorbias. The village occupies a shallow, irregular 10-square-foot basin filled with a mix of one-third garden soil, one-third pumice, and one-third cactus mix. Inspired by designer Gary Bartl's Sierrascapes, I positioned triangular flagstones for a backdrop suggestive of mountain peaks.

Succulents for Miniature Landscapes

In my own miniature garden, dark green *Haworthia limifolia* rosettes represent agaves, and cuttings of devil's backbone (*Pedilanthus tithymaloides* 'Variegata') with zigzag stems suggest ocotillo. Small stapeliads (columnar cacti) and *Euphorbia anoplia* resemble ceroid (columnar) cacti and will produce new stems or offsets without getting overly large.

These small succulents are useful for suggesting much larger ones:

- Dwarf cultivars of aloe and sansevieria, as well as *Euphorbia milii* (resemble their larger counterparts)

- *Euphorbia anoplia, E. enopla, E. mammilaris*, cuttings of *E. tirucalli*, and stapeliads (columnar cacti)

- *Euphorbia pulvinata* 'Nana', dwarf form; *Mammillaria gracilis* 'Fragilis' (spherical cacti)

- Haworthias with pointed tips such as *H. attenuata* and *H. limifolia* (agaves)

- *Opuntia rufida* 'Desert Gem' (paddle-leaved cacti)

- *Pedilanthus tithymaloides* (devil's backbone, an ocotillo)

To suggest fine-leaved shrubs and minitrees, use cuttings of one or more of these or obtain the plants in small pots:

- *Aeonium* 'Kiwi'

- *Crassula* 'Irish Bouquet'

- *Crassula ovata* 'Gollum'

- *Crassula muscosa* (watch-chain crassula)

- *Crassula sarcocaulis* (bonsai crassula)

- *Crassula tetragona*

- *Echeveria* species that branch (such as *E. harmsii*)

- ice plants

- *Kalanchoe blossfeldiana* (supermarket kalanchoe)

- *Kalanchoe tomentosa* (panda plant)

- living stones (succulents in these genera: *Argyroderma, Conophytum, Fenestraria, Lithops*, and *Pleiospilos*)

- *Othonna capensis* (little pickles)

The largest hides an irrigation riser that waters the bank behind it. Water percolates downward, keeping the soil of the miniature landscape moist. Its cacti and small succulents are thereby watered by osmosis and receive no direct irrigation. The "creek" alongside the steps doesn't function as a water source but rather suggests one, an illusion I enhanced by strewing it with florist's marbles and sparkly bits of tumbled glass. The scene's focal point, a one-dimensional painted plaster cathedral, was a lucky find at a thrift store.

I planted the slope with a forest of *Crassula tetragona* cuttings and *Sedum rupestre* 'Blue Spruce' (also sold as *S. reflexum* 'Blue Spruce'). A small mirror set in sand creates a lake at the creek's terminus. A pile of tiny gears, screws, and other odds and ends at lower left, between buildings and road, serves as a landfill.

Flowerpots no bigger than thimbles hold *Aeonium* 'Kiwi' rosettes—cuttings that will last a week or more without water. In the foreground is *Sedum makinoi* 'Ogon'; at right, *Echeveria harmsii* rosettes.

- *Sedum*, tiny-leaved varieties: leaves of *S. dasyphyllum* and *S. ×rubrotinctum* 'Mini' resemble grains of rice; *S. rupestre* 'Angelina' and 'Blue Spruce' appear bristly; and *S. spathulifolium* 'Cape Blanco' and *S. spurium* 'Dragon's Blood' form tiny rosettes. *Sedum makinoi* 'Ogon' (rounded leaves) and *S. acre* (pointed leaves) range from bright chartreuse to shades of yellow.

- *Senecio serpens*

- *Senecio vitalis*

Imaginary visitors trekking to the Central American village in my garden traverse a rocky wilderness. The red-roofed house at lower left is the vacation home of *norteamericanos* who consider the village (as I do) a remote getaway untouched by civilization.

Success Secrets
for Succulents

OPPOSITE Plantlets along the leaves of *Kalanchoe laetivirens*, a bryophyllum, are ready to drop off and take root.

PREVIOUS SPREAD Perfectly grown cacti in Peter Walkowiak's collection are often on display at meetings and shows where enthusiasts gather: southern California affiliates of the Cactus and Succulent Society of America.

To keep your succulent garden looking good year-round with minimal effort, heed the following suggestions for planting, watering, and grooming; protecting your succulents from diseases, pests, and weather damage; and assuring a continuing supply of new plants by propagating existing ones.

My garden tools include a trowel, tongs for grasping cactus, 70 percent alcohol for spraying aphids and mealies, clippers for fine pruning, a small screwdriver for adjusting irrigation sprayers, a sun visor, leather gloves, Felco pruners, two pairs of pliers (one for holding a riser, the other for unscrewing the head), long tweezers for reaching where my fingers can't, a soil knife for cutting roots, and a serrated kitchen knife for sawing through soft limbs (such as those of yuccas).

Hybridizer Kelly Griffin's garden

Among succulent collectors, plant breeder Kelly Griffin's name is spoken with reverence. The aloes and agaves Griffin has hybridized are unusual, colorful, and highly sought after—which has earned him the enviable job of breeding plants for a living and traveling to remote regions to discover new ones. As manager of succulent plant development at Altman Plants in Vista, California, the largest grower of cacti and succulents in the United States, he has gone on expeditions to South Africa, Madagascar, Yemen, Colombia, Argentina, Chile, Peru, and twenty-six of the thirty-one states of Mexico. Griffin's goal is to hybridize new and better succulents that exhibit desirable characteristics of both parents. He's known for creating dwarf aloes and the popular landscape agave 'Blue Glow'.

Griffin's own garden near San Diego is a testing ground for plants that have caught his fancy and hybrids he's created that have yet to be released into the nursery marketplace. He's captivated by variegation, which he describes as "a mutation that causes a weakness because of a lack of chlorophyll," giving a plant striped, streaked, or mottled leaves. Variegation is especially desirable in agaves, he notes, grown as they are for their foliage and not their flowers. He points out that variegated agaves are a great choice because in addition to their beauty, they aren't as robust as their solid green cousins and are therefore less likely to take over a garden.

Griffin landscaped his garden with "the plants that I love—aloes, dudleyas, and agaves." He started most of them from seed, then planted them in the garden when small. "Visitors are sometimes surprised that you can grow large succulents from seeds," he says, "but yes, of course, you can grow any plant from a seed. That's how plants exist. Somewhere in the world, everything you see here is a weed. Putting certain weeds together makes a nice garden." His was two years old when I visited and photographed it.

Griffin has a keen interest in succulents in the genus *Dudleya*, which are native to coastal and Baja California. He's enthusiastic about a hybrid (lower left) he created by crossing *D. pulverulenta* and *D. brittonii*. Among its desirable traits are abundant, long-lasting flower clusters atop tall stalks.

The majority of plants in Griffin's garden are unnamed hybrids. Mounded soil enhances drainage and elevates plants for better viewing.

LEFT Griffin uses a ladder to access an agave's bloom spike. He's checking the progress of seed capsules resulting from flowers he dusted with pollen from a different variety.

BELOW A rare variegated *Agave bovicornuta* enhances Griffin's garden.

Instead of trying to slide an *Agave guiengola* out of its nursery pot—which might have broken the top of the plant away from its roots—landscapers sliced the pot open with an ax. The next step is to spread and prune the plant's coiled roots.

Planting Tips and Techniques

Before you plant, spade compacted soil to loosen it so roots will penetrate easily. When you transplant a succulent from its nursery pot, dig a hole deep enough to cover its roots once they have been freed from the pot and untangled. Elevate the crown slightly to compensate for sinking later on. As soon as the plant is situated, tamp the dirt around its base and then water well to settle the roots. (An exception is cactus, which shouldn't be watered until damaged roots have a chance to heal, lest they rot. Give newly transplanted cacti four to six weeks to settle in before watering them.)

When planting succulent ground covers from nursery flats, use a trowel to dig holes several inches deep and about a foot apart. Separate the plants, insert one into each hole, and press loose soil gently around the roots to anchor them.

If you're working with any large spiny or prickly plant, wear elbow-length leather gloves and eye protection. The latter is especially important if you're dealing with paddle cacti (those in the genus *Opuntia*) covered with glochids. Even if you don't touch them, the tiny, translucent, furlike spines can become airborne. Some cactus aficionados buy inexpensive leather gardening gloves (in quantity to get the best price), then discard them when coated with spines. You can also wrap the fingers and palms of rubber garden gloves with duct tape, which glochids don't seem to penetrate. To carry a small cactus, wrap it with a towel folded so that you can lift the plant with the ends, or grasp it with kitchen tongs. If tongs might harm the plant, pad the tips with small blocks of foam rubber secured with rubber bands.

Succulents that are large (several feet high and equally wide) can be surprisingly heavy. Lifting and moving them is a two-person job, even with the help of a dolly or wheeled cart. Professional landscapers and nurserymen transport "armed and dangerous" succulents by wrapping them in carpet remnants; by rolling them onto a blanket or beach towel, which serves as a sling; or by carrying the plant on a stretcher constructed of rigid boards that support the plant's weight. Though it takes two to lift it, a stretcher is better than a wheelbarrow, because it can be placed on the ground next to the plant, which then is slid onto it.

LEFT As he transplants a small paddle cactus, succulent enthusiast Matthew Wong, age twelve, holds it with salad tongs.

BOTTOM, LEFT When my friend Elisabeth Crouch transplants a barrel cactus, she grasps the roots with one gloved hand and with the other, cushions the plant with folded newspaper. Behind her are silver torch cacti (*Cleistocactus strausii*) postbloom.

BELOW To dig up and move a barrel cactus, use a shovel to uproot the plant, then loop a soft hose around it so you can lift and carry it without damaging it—or having it damage you.

As plants grow, the location of fixed irrigation risers and the quantity and direction of their spray should be adjusted accordingly.

Water and Fertilizer

Everyone, it seems, is concerned about overwatering succulents. To reassure you, the guidelines here are simple and based on common sense. (Also see "Succulents A to Z" for information about the water needs of specific types of plants.)

Regardless of their size or variety, if your succulents are watered thoroughly (by you or by rainfall) once a week in summer, twice a month in spring and fall, and once a month in winter, they'll probably do fine, provided you keep in mind these important variables: temperature, humidity, sun exposure, type of plant, and soil porosity and depth. Ideally, soil several inches below the surface stays about as moist as a wrung-out sponge. This enables fine, hairlike roots to keep hydrated. If these desiccate, as sometimes happens in the plants' native habitats, growth ceases. Young or delicate-leaved succulents may not survive, but tougher ones will send forth new roots when watered again (that is, when you or the rains return).

The fatter the succulent, the more camel-like it is and the less water it requires. The corollary to this is that the thicker and juicier the leaves, the more vulnerable it is to overwatering—which is especially true of

To ensure that rot-prone succulents such as cacti aren't overwatered, plant them higher than their thirstier neighbors.

cacti and rotund euphorbias. Large and mature specimens of cactus, yucca, dasylirion, agave, jade plant, *Portulacaria afra*, and aloe can go months, even years, with no water other than rainfall. However, during prolonged dry spells, they do appreciate an occasional deep soaking (every four to six weeks). Let a hose drip overnight at the base of the plant or slightly uphill from it.

During dormancy, which for most succulents is winter, the plants don't require much water. In California's banana belt for succulents, this means decreasing irrigation in October and withholding it from November through March. This is also the region's rainy season, which typically averages 15 inches—an ideal amount, especially when evenly spaced, to encourage root formation that will boost new growth in spring.

Annually in your garden right before a winter rainstorm, spread Ironite according to package directions. Avoid letting granules land in rosettes or on hardscape, because they can leave rust stains. In spring, as succulents awaken from dormancy, apply a balanced granular fertilizer. March or April is also the best time to feed container-grown succulents; I give mine a tea made from composted, dehydrated cow manure.

Not all succulents are winter dormant; a few slow down in summer. Those that are committed winter growers, like *Dracaena draco*, do well with no summer watering at all, while others—notably aeoniums—merely rest in summer and should be given just enough water to prevent desiccation.

Test your irrigation system from time to time to evaluate its efficiency. Check drip emitters to make sure they're not clogged, and prune any new growth that blocks sprayers. Because plants need no water during storms and may require more during hot, dry spells, evaluate the settings (frequency and duration) several times a year. If the system doesn't detect precipitation and shut itself off, acquire the habit of turning it off when rain is predicted.

My garden's automatic irrigation is set to run before sunrise, seven minutes once a week, from April through October. The system also fills a birdbath. If the birdbath goes dry between weekly waterings, I know the soil is dry, too, and I give vulnerable plants supplemental water. I use a hose with a trigger sprayer so water goes only where it's needed.

OPPOSITE, TOP In autumn as they're waking from summer dormancy, prune leggy aeoniums, remove dry lower leaves, freshen the soil, and plant the cuttings. New roots will form along the stems where leaves were attached. Discard old plants and roots.

OPPOSITE, BOTTOM *Agave* 'Blue Flame' has needlelike tips that can be snipped to make them less treacherous.

Grooming Your Succulents

What little care and maintenance my hundreds of succulents require takes two to four hours a week of my time. Tasks include the following:

Remove debris If you're not under water restrictions, a blast of water from a hose helps to clean leaves and dirt from the center of rosette succulents. Long tweezers also do the job. When it comes to large agaves, yuccas, and other sharp-leaved succulents, I use a leaf blower (electric, which is less noisy than battery powered) or flick debris from the plants' leaf axils with a long wooden dowel.

Deadhead Snip spent flower stalks where they emerge from the plant.

Morticia prune The fictional character Morticia Addams of the Addams Family would cut and discard healthy roses. Her reasons were aesthetic; mine are practical. Blooms of fancy echeverias, certain stacked crassulas, and *Kalanchoe luciae* draw so much energy from the plants they can weaken them or spoil their shape. (There's no point in cutting the blooms off of agaves and aeoniums; they'll die regardless.) A few other succulents, including haworthias and senecios, have insignificant flowers that are spindly or resemble dandelions, so I remove them as well.

Trim leggy plants and start cuttings When aeonium trunks attain 12 inches high or more, cut the rosettes several inches below the lowest leaves and replant. Do this twice a year to keep *Senecio mandraliscae* looking good, too. It branches when cut, creating a more lush and less lanky ground cover. Plant the tips in bare areas and discard the leafless stems.

Blunt sharp agave tips Remove a quarter inch from the tips of agaves planted where their spines might endanger passersby, especially children or pets who get too close.

Peel away dead leaves Dry lower leaves of rosette succulents persist and can look untidy. They provide protection from sunburn and frost, so I generally (and lazily) leave them be. But if you find them unsightly, peel them away.

Trim damaged leaves Frost and excessive sun can turn leaf edges pale and crisp. Make the plants look better instantly by cutting the damaged tissue to a curve or point—whatever the leaf's shape would naturally be.

Patrol for pups Watch for pups that pop up near aloes and agaves and remove them if unwanted. Plant elsewhere or set them aside to give to friends and garden visitors.

Check for pests and weeds Be vigilant, get them early, and treat immediately.

Pest and Damage Control

Sometimes it may seem that your garden is Pandora's box, a haven for pests whose mission is to seek and destroy. Fortunately, succulents are tough, and damage

Echeveria buds damaged by aphids may not open. The black specks are mature insects; the white ones, newly hatched grubs.

Scale covers the pads of a dwarf opuntia. When an infestation is this severe, there's little point in trying to save the plant.

can be curbed. I've tackled—and overcome—threats that range from microscopic mites to mammals. Following are the preventive measures I recommend and my environmentally friendly methods of control.

Harmful insects

Especially if air circulation is inadequate, succulents that send forth tender new growth and buds are vulnerable to tiny sucking insects that once ensconced proliferate rapidly and are difficult to get rid of. Mealybugs look like bits of cotton fluff; scale shows up as hard, oval brown bumps; and aphids, thrips, and spider mites are soft-bodied insects that latch onto and consume new tissue. Mealybugs lodge in leaf axils (where leaves join the stem); similar in appearance are white aphids that may infest roots. Scale is typically found on stems.

Prevention is ideal; immediate treatment, imperative. At the first sign of infestation, container-grown plants should be quarantined. Those severely affected should be bagged and set out with the trash, lest the pests move on to healthy plants. Discard the potting soil and wash the container thoroughly before reusing it.

I keep isopropyl rubbing alcohol (labeled "70 percent") handy in a spray bottle, ready to go at the first sign of a problem. A fine, light spray of alcohol does no damage to succulent leaves and kills soft-bodied insects instantly. Scale is more persistent.

Improved, ultrarefined ("superior") horticultural oils and insecticidal soaps are easy on us, our pets, and the earth. When applied according to label directions, oils and soaps are effective against spider mites, aphids, scale, and whiteflies. Oils smother insects and their eggs; soaps disrupt their membranes. (Dish soap isn't as effective and can damage plants.) Hose the plant to dislodge as many pests as possible, then treat both sides of the leaves and leaf axils—wherever pests might hide. For an effective, nontoxic fungicide, mix baking soda with horticultural oil per label directions. Also check the label for lists of plants *not* to spray. When a succulent's color is the result of a powdery or waxy coating on its leaves, oil or alcohol may remove it, leaving it merely green. If in doubt, try a small area and wait twenty-four hours to see if any damage develops.

Aloe mites cause unsightly, cancerous growth.

Aloes are prone to aloe mite, a microscopic insect that causes lumpy and distorted growth in leaf axils, along the edges of leaves, and sometimes in the blooms. Unfortunately, no cure is known, and affected plants or portions thereof should be removed and destroyed to protect nearby aloes. Also clean and disinfect any tools that may have touched diseased tissue.

Check your in-ground agaves for brown puncture holes in their central cones. This is one sign of agave snout weevil infestation, as are plants that wobble when pushed, have darkened tissue at leaf axils, and have floppy lower leaves. The snout nose weevil is a half-inch-long black beetle that is most active in the spring. It pierces an agave's core, injects microbes that soften tissues, and then lays eggs in the hole. Grubs consume the heart of the plant before burrowing into the ground to pupate. Affected agaves eventually collapse. If you've had an infestation or hear of one in your area, keep an eye on your existing agaves and plant new ones bare root only, or in pots atop hardscape. At first sign, remove and destroy the agave. It won't recover, and you're feeding weevils if you keep it. Also get rid of infested soil

Variegates of *Agave americana* are a favorite of agave snout nose weevils.

and don't plant agaves in that location again. Beetles (which can't fly) and grubs usually arrive via new plants. Remove agaves from their nursery pots, set the plants in a wheelbarrow, examine leaf axils for weevils, and hose the roots as you check for grubs. Should pests be present, dispose of soil and agaves, and notify the source. Species known to be susceptible include *Agave weberi*, *A. americana*, *A. parryi*, and *A. angustifolia*. The weevil also attacks other plants in the family Agaveaceae, such as those in genera *Beaucarnea*, *Dasylirion*, and *Yucca*, and certain cacti, notably Mexican fence post (*Pachycereus marginatus*).

How to combat ants and mealybugs

Ants spread mealybugs, scale, aphids, and other pests, and target the tender cores of echeverias, haworthias, gasterias, and small aloes. One sign that ants are at work is that plants' centers are filled with soil. This often happens in late summer, when succulents are stressed by heat and ants are looking for moisture and winter lodgings.

To treat an infested plant, follow these steps:

1. Isolate the plant so the pests don't spread.

2. Clean the area surrounding it to get rid of any bugs or eggs hiding in cracks and crevices.

3. Remove the plant from its pot or the ground and check the roots. If they're infested, remove most of them.

4. Hose the plant, roots and all, to clean it. If it's salvageable (leaves firmly attached to the stem or core), treat it with a mix of insecticidal soap and horticultural oil per label directions.

5. Keep the plant out of direct sun. Wait several days and reapply the solution.

6. Take cuttings (optional). If the mother plant continues to be targeted by pests and you have to discard it, its offspring may fare better.

7. Replant in fresh soil or potting mix. Start any cuttings separately. Keep an eye on them for several weeks before returning them to the garden or your collection.

8. Routinely examine leaf axils. At the first sign pests have returned, repeat the process.

To keep ants from colonizing potted plants, place a piece of plastic window screen over the drain hole at planting time before adding soil. Plants already potted can be set atop a metal stand in a saucer of water. Fill the moat daily or when dry.

What looks like coffee grounds in the center of a succulent rosette is soil deposited by ants.

There was no saving this gopher-eaten agave with its meristem (the region of cells that give rise to division and growth) destroyed.

Gophers

Gophers are rat-size, burrowing animals that breed in spring. Their activity is evidenced by 6-inch-high mounds of fresh soil that result from digging and tunnel excavation. Although they prefer the roots of fruit-producing trees and herbs, gophers also go after numerous other plants. Among succulents, gophers especially like variegated agaves.

Over the years, I've tried everything from flooding gopher runs to smoking them out with automotive flares and have found nothing as effective as traps similar to those my father used in his avocado orchard (one brand is Macabee). They're made of heavy gauge wire and somewhat resemble rat traps. On average every spring, I midwife three to five gophers from my garden. It takes me one to three attempts to successfully catch a gopher, a percentage I'm proud of.

Snails

Snails reproduce in abundance in wet weather and unless stopped chew unsightly holes in plants—a tragedy for succulents because they have relatively few leaves and keep them a long time. The least expensive method of control is handpicking, best done on a drizzly day by children who find it fun (and are paid per snail). Baits and predator snails are more effective, but they do need to be reapplied or reintroduced when the pest snail population resurges (and it always does). Use only environmentally friendly baits (such as Sluggo), which are safe around pets and wildlife because the active ingredient, iron phosphate, is a naturally occurring plant nutrient that affects only mollusks.

Decollate (predator) snails are another option. They're about an inch long and resemble conical seashells; inside is a slender black gastropod with an appetite for immature spherical (helix) snails and their eggs. Decollates leave the largest helix snails alone, so you'll still have to handpick them, or bait for them six weeks before releasing decollates. They're approved in some regions but not in others (such as California north of Santa Barbara) for fear they'll disrupt the ecological balance. Not that much seems in balance anymore; helix snails, for example, are not native. One theory is that they were introduced as a potential human food source. Indeed, that's the only control measure I've yet to try.

A brown helix snail exits the scene of the crime.

Weed Control

Weeds sprout wherever soil is exposed to sunlight. Succulent ground covers work well to keep weeds under control but take time to fill in—hence the need for an inorganic topdressing to cover bare areas. The deeper the layer of crushed rock, the easier those few weeds that sprout will be to pull, because their roots aren't cemented into hard soil.

In spring, be vigilant and hoe bare dirt as soon as you see uninvited slivers of green. At that point, weeds are young, tender, and lightly rooted. In areas where a hoe is too large, disturb the soil with a trowel, steel file, or spackling knife. This may seem tedious, but the larger a weed gets, the more difficult it is to remove. I sometimes use boiling water to kill weeds in cracks and crevices, and long tweezers or hemostats to pull those amid spiny agaves and cacti.

If the task of eliminating annual weeds is overwhelming, at least remove their flower buds or seed heads. This is more important than uprooting the plant, which you can do later; or you can simply let the weed die at the end of its growth cycle. (In fact, if erosion is a concern, roots of annual weeds should be left in the soil.) Let weeds go to seed, and you'll contend with their offspring the following year.

Bag all weeds and send them out with the trash, or put them in your yard debris bin. Don't leave them on the ground or add them to your compost pile.

Cultivating Succulents in Challenging Climates

The secret of caring for any plant is to understand its native habitat and try to replicate that as much as possible in your garden, greenhouse, or home. Succulents by and large come from warm, dry regions with low humidity (the drier the better) and minimal rainfall (fewer than 20 inches per year). The preferred temperature range for nonhardy succulents is 40 to 85°F. Most need protection from scorching sun, excessive rainfall, high humidity, and freezing temperatures. Following are tips for growing healthy succulents in climates that are outside the plants' natural comfort range.

I claim the dubious distinction of having been outwitted by a weed. Touch a ripe seedpod of wood sorrel, a type of oxalis, and it spins open, shooting seeds several feet. I found this fascinating and fun to show visitors, so I let the plant live. It's been laughing at me ever since.

The art of stressing succulents

Ideal conditions for *Sedum rupestre* 'Angelina' (lower right) must be somewhat stressful for the kalanchoe alongside it; otherwise its leaves would be larger and lose their blush.

Most aloes and crassulas plus certain kalanchoes, euphorbias, sempervivums, sedums, aeoniums, and echeverias turn vibrant colors when stressed (grown in less-than-ideal conditions). Protective chemicals in the leaves produce hues of red, yellow, orange, and purple. If a succulent's leaves are margined or tipped in a contrasting hue, stress will likely enhance that color. Because leaves of stressed plants tend to be smaller than those of their pampered green counterparts, stressed plants are often more compact.

There's no exact formula for stressing a succulent, so it comes down to trial and error. It's often the difference between growing the plants "soft," meaning with regular water, rich soil, consistent fertilizer, and filtered light, or "hard" as in nature, with extremes of heat or cold, strong sun, nutrient-deficient soil, and inconsistent moisture. Of course, if you stress a succulent too much, it may not recover. If leaf tips have shriveled and turned beige or gray, the plant is suffering and needs a kinder location. If a plant reddens unexpectedly,

These 'Sunset' jade plants were indistinguishable until I placed the one on the left in less sun. Six weeks later, it had reverted to green and its leaves were bigger, its stems longer, and its form less compact.

its roots may be unable to access moisture and nutrients due to rot, desiccation, or infestation.

Vividly hued succulents have more commercial value than green ones, so succulent specialty nurseries are pros at stressing plants. When you buy a beauty, observe where it was in the nursery—especially the amount and duration of light it received—and then replicate that at home.

A shade structure at the Desert Botanical Garden in Phoenix protects young cacti from sunburn and desiccation.

Desert climates

Desert regions tend to be too hot and too cold to grow those succulents I call "the pretty little ones" (echeverias, aeoniums, euphorbias, kalanchoes, sempervivums, and crassulas), at least out in the open. However, you can create a beautiful desert garden with agaves (and there are dozens of varieties, from diminutive to immense), as well as dasylirions, hesperaloes, *Portulacaria afra*, yuccas, and cacti.

To prevent such succulents from being scorched by strong sun when young (or if soft-leaved, at any age), grow them beneath shade cloth or in the dappled light of a desert-adapted tree such as palo verde. Move container-grown specimens into bright shade when daytime temperatures rise above 90°F and during monsoonal rains (lest the roots rot).

During long dry spells, many desert succulents go dormant and close their rosettes (or, if ribbed, shrink in size), and their roots shrivel. When the rains—or you, wielding a hose—come again, they absorb moisture and expand, thereby exposing more of their surface area to the sun. Increased photosynthesis (a process that happens when chlorophyll meets sunlight) fuels new growth.

Rainy and humid climates

Succulents may rot if grown in water-retentive soil in regions with annual rainfall in excess of 20 inches. Decay that affects waterlogged roots moves upward into the plant's stem or trunk, which softens and collapses. Succulents that are especially at risk, such as cacti, are best grown in pure pumice or a mix of pumice and

It's not water that causes roots to rot but lack of oxygen (plus microbes). *Agave attenuata* (shown here), crassulas, yuccas, and other succulents thrive in Hilo, Hawaii, where precipitation averages 200+ inches a year. Although rain bathes the roots continually, they stay aerated and healthy because the soil is fast-draining, porous lava rock.

coarse sand, such as decomposed granite. Fungus or bacteria in organic matter that falls into the crowns of succulents can also cause rot, so keep your succulents and the ground around them free of decaying leaves.

Should rot happen, take cuttings from healthy top growth and restart the plants—as I did with aeoniums after an El Niño winter. Despite double normal rainfall, the rest of my succulents were fine, thanks to fast-draining soil. (The native soil is decomposed granite, which in most garden beds I've amended with pumice and compost. The garden's sloping terrain also enhances drainage.)

It's best to avoid planting in depressions or basins, but if succulents do occupy low-lying areas of your garden and you don't want to move the plants to higher ground, protect them with a patio umbrella or a makeshift shelter during storms. (Keep in mind that wind-driven rain falls at an angle, not perpendicular to the ground.) Channel runoff with rocks, sandbags, or trenches; and top-dress soggy soil with pumice to absorb standing water.

When they stay damp, succulents from arid regions are prone to insect and fungal infestations. If you live in a warm, humid climate, give the plants good light and air circulation, and—if they're indoors—a dehumidifier. Or cultivate succulents from tropical latitudes instead, such as those in the genera *Epiphyllum, Hatiora, Hoya, Lepismium, Schlumbergera,* and *Rhipsalis.* These understory plants with pendant stems thrive in bright shade and hanging baskets.

Succulents for outdoor tropical gardens include *Agave attenuata, Aloe arborescens, Cotyledon orbiculata, Crassula ovata, Euphorbia milii, Furcraea foetida, Kalanchoe blossfeldiana, K. luciae, K. prolifera,* peperomias, *Pachypodium lamerei,* and sansevierias. All need frost protection and do best in full sun for half the day, ideally morning. (Some species of opuntia, *Carpobrotus edulis,* and kalanchoes in the subcategory bryophyllum also thrive in tropical climates but aren't recommended because they may become invasive.)

Areas with frost

Water expands when it freezes, which can burst the walls of plant cells and turn succulents to mush. Those that are frost tolerant can handle the formation of ice crystals within their cells or have salts in cellular fluids that lower the temperature at which they freeze. Keeping tender succulents on the dry side during colder months helps to decrease their moisture content and increase the salt-to-water ratio of cellular fluid.

Weather that is most threatening to succulents is rain followed by frost, because cells are engorged. New growth is particularly at risk. Often—particularly with aloes—the tips of leaves freeze, but the rest of the plant is fine. These tips remain dry and shriveled, which doesn't harm the plant but may compromise its appearance. If top growth has frozen but roots are still viable, certain succulents will regrow; among them are *Kalanchoe luciae,* perennial shrub sedums (such as 'Autumn Joy'), *Aloe maculata, Bulbine frutescens,* yuccas, pup-forming agaves, and any with an underground caudex (bulbous stem).

If you reside, as I do, where frosts are mild (temps seldom lower than 27°F) and brief (fewer than two hours), you can cultivate tender succulents in the ground year-round—provided you grow them in your garden's warmer microclimates and move or cover vulnerable plants when frost threatens. A tree branch, patio umbrella, or bedsheet will protect succulents beneath it by lessening the dissipation of soil warmth and preventing ice crystals from landing on leaves.

Frost cloth and floating row covers, sold at garden centers in rolls 5 to 6 feet wide and up to 375 feet long, afford protection from frost and can be reused. Keep the lightweight, translucent fabric in place with stones so wind won't dislodge it. In areas with consistently frosty nights, row covers can be left on all winter. Never cover plants with plastic, which traps moisture and intensifies the heat of the sun—a combination that can be more harmful than frost. Also avoid any material so heavy it might break or crease leaves, causing permanent damage.

If you live in zone 8 or below, grow cold-hardy succulents (see the section on these in "Specialty Gardens That Showcase Succulents"). Move tender succulents indoors in autumn or grow them as annuals that you replace from one year to the next. What you decide to do depends on how gung-ho a gardener you are.

To protect your succulents from sustained cold or particularly low temps, you'll need a well-ventilated shelter that stays above 32°F. Sleeping succulents are gearing up to bloom in spring, and many won't do so without several weeks below 55°F. Since this is much colder than you're likely to be comfortable with, overwintering plants in your basement or a separate structure is likely best for both of you.

Every region has its own challenges. Before you build a lean-to alongside your house or invest in a greenhouse, ask members of the nearest chapter of the Cactus and Succulent Society of America for advice and

Frost cloth protects an agave in the Ruth Bancroft Garden in Walnut Creek, California.

To diminish the intensity of late afternoon sun, shade cloth covers a greenhouse's west-facing windows. Hinged panes along the ridgeline allow hot air to escape. A pet door, lower left, lets the structure double as a doghouse on chilly nights.

recommendations. Be sure to research the best orientation of the greenhouse to the sun.

Dormant plants don't need a full-spectrum light source, and fluorescent is the most economical. When programmed to shine six hours daily, the light ensures the plants' health and prevents etiolated (stretched) growth.

Potted succulents are obviously easier to move indoors than those in the ground. However, it's not difficult to scoop shallow-rooted succulents (such as echeverias and crassulas) from garden beds and pack them into nursery flats. (Check for insects, snails, and other pests you don't want to keep snug all winter.) Another option is to harvest cuttings or divisions in autumn, root them indoors in pots or flats during the winter, and then plant them outdoors when the weather warms.

In spring, when you're ready to reintroduce your succulents to the garden, acclimatize them gradually to outside temperatures and the sun's ultraviolet rays. The best time to transition your potted succulents to the outdoors is during mild, cloudy weather. If sun is the norm, place the plants in bright shade, leave them there a few days, and then give them a little more sun daily.

Propagation:
New Plants from Old

Succulents are easier to propagate than perhaps any other type of plant. If you study a succulent, how it reproduces will often become obvious. Leaves that detach easily, for example, are capable of sending forth roots and new little plants. Stems sometimes produce whiskery roots along their undersides where leaves were once attached. To launch a new plant, do what the parent plant is asking: cut the stem and bury the aerial roots.

The best time to propagate winter-dormant succulents (the majority) is in spring, as they begin their active growth cycle and before summer heat intensifies. Start summer-dormant succulents—such as aeoniums, dudleyas, othonnas, and certain senecios and crassulas—in autumn.

Leaf propagation

Numerous succulents—among them graptopetalums, gasterias, pachyphytums, graptoverias, pachyverias, sedums, kalanchoes, and some echeverias and crassulas—produce new plants from fallen leaves. Beneath the mother plant, they're sheltered from hot sun and find soil and moisture in which to root. To start a lot of new little plants, line a nursery tray with weed cloth, screen,

Meristem (or meristematic) tissue along an aeonium's trunk exists at the centers of what look like potato eyes. The growth cells produce both leaves and roots.

New leaves and roots grow from the stem end of a graptoveria leaf.

×*Graptosedum* 'California Sunset' leaves strewn atop a flat filled mostly with pumice have produced small plants.

or paper towels (so soil won't fall through gaps), fill the tray nearly full with coarse potting mix, and lay leaves atop it about an inch apart. Keep the tray out of direct sun and don't water it until leaves have rooted, lest they rot.

To pot up a succulent you started via leaf propagation, wait until the new little plant has formed leaves and threadlike roots; this happens as it drains moisture and nutrients from the mother leaf, which will shrivel. As you would any newly potted plant, protect it from strong sun until well established.

Cuttings

To start succulents from cuttings, cleanly cut several inches of stem below the topmost leaves using garden shears, scissors, or a sharp knife. If the cut is raw and juicy, give it several days to heal—the end will callus over—before planting. Although some experts recommend dipping stems into sulphur to discourage fungus or into rooting hormone to promote cellular growth, I haven't noticed that either makes a difference. What does help is keeping the cuttings upright. Influenced by gravity, internal root-promoting hormones gather in tissue nearest the ground.

If you delay planting succulent cuttings, after a week or so roots may grow anyway—into thin air. When severed from the mother plant, cuttings reverse the flow of growth, sending nutrients from stems and leaves into root formation.

Whether in garden beds, nursery flats, or containers, cuttings will get off to a good start in a mixture of a third potting soil, a third sharp sand, and a third pumice. If there's a high risk of rotting, increase the percentage of pumice. Water only enough to keep the mix moist; growers often keep a spray bottle handy. If the cutting rots at the base before roots form, cut tissue higher up, let the raw end callus, and replant in fresh soil. Keep cuttings in bright shade until rooted (firmly in place when nudged). Columnar and jointed succulents (like cholla cactus) are easy to propagate; simply place a piece upright in potting mix and keep on the dry side until roots form. When handling cuttings from euphorbias, wear gloves and eye protection; the milky sap is caustic.

Once young plants are well rooted, transplant them into the garden. For the first week or so, shade them with empty nursery flats or dry, twiggy tree branches. Or simply position a piece of garden furniture between the plants and midday sun.

Sedum ×*rubrotinctum* 'Pork and Beans' starts readily from cuttings. Leaves, which pop off easily, may root as well.

Grandma Lola:
An experiment in delayed planting

In June 2015 I finally planted a cutting taken three years earlier. I waited because I was curious how long it would remain viable without soil or water. The three-year-old cutting's rosette was smaller and greener than its original silvery pink, the stem was longer, and there were more dry leaves as well as new ones. The photos illustrate the chronology.

June 2012: This is one of five *Echeveria* 'Lola' rosettes that were wired onto floral picks and photographed for the how-to project on page 167 of my book *Succulents Simplified* (Timber Press, 2013). Afterward, I set them in an empty vase on my deck out of direct sunlight.

ABOVE June 2013: A year later, the Lolas had fueled new growth by cannibalizing their older leaves, which though crisp and withered still clung to the stems. Some of the wrinkled leaves sheltered pink, threadlike roots. I named the largest rosette Grandma. Ensconced in a padded shoebox, Grandma accompanied me to several succulent events so that others could also marvel at her longevity. In the fall of 2014, mealybugs attempted an infestation, but after a shot of alcohol, Grandma and her friends were fine.

RIGHT In the summer of 2015, the bouquet accidentally received too much sun, and Grandma's leaves were scorched. That autumn, I peeled away her dry lower leaves, snipped her stem, and planted her in a 4-inch pot. The sole Lola remaining atop a floral pick is shown here with Grandma (newly rooted) in December 2015. The two occupy a sheltered, bright-shade location where I'll keep an eye on them—unless, of course, they outlive me.

My neighbor's San Pedro cactus (*Echinopsis pachanoi*) exhibits new growth where stems were cut.

These *Agave americana* 'Marginata' plants are young, but their rhizomatous roots have already spawned pups.

Division, plantlets, and offsets

Uprooting (or unpotting) an overgrown plant and pulling its stems and roots apart is called division. Sometimes roots are so dense and tangled they have to be separated with a saw—often the case with overgrown sansevierias. Divide offsets by cutting or wiggling them loose from the parent, and then peel away any old, dry leaves. When you plant the offspring, space them so they'll have room to reproduce on their own.

Rhizomes are fleshy underground roots from which new plants sprout. These pups are a bonus if you want them and a nuisance if you don't. In any case, propagation is easy: simply dig up the new plant, and it's ready to restart elsewhere. *Agave americana* launches vigorous rhizomes laterally under the soil, which soon results in a cluster of smaller pups nestled at its base. I've seen pups pop up several feet from the mother plant, which seems to look the other way, as though saying, "Those aren't mine!"

A few years ago, a neighbor sliced a 6-foot-tall columnar cactus in half horizontally. After the top part lay on the ground a few days, he planted it alongside the other. A pair of green poles? What was he thinking!

A month or so later, he cut the newly planted piece in half horizontally and repeated the process. Meanwhile, two tiny miniatures of the original cactus had appeared on either side of its healed top, which resembled a seven-pointed star. What was once a solo ceroid is now a multilevel colony of various-sized offspring that enhances his front yard.

Certain succulents produce new little plants on their bloom spikes infrequently—haworthias and graptoverias come to mind—but others do it consistently, in particular *Kalanchoe synsepala* and *Crassula multicava*. When an offset nourished by a flower stem gets heavy enough, it touches the ground. The juvenile, having formed aerial roots, thereby establishes itself a foot or more from its parent.

Kalanchoes in the subcategory bryophyllum form plantlets along their scalloped leaf margins, giving them a ruffled look; these drop by the dozens and take root. Some gardeners consider such abundance a problem, and indeed it can be. On the plus side, if these young plants are allowed to mature, they produce lovely parasols of bell-shaped flowers.

When an agave flowers

It can take years—sometimes decades, depending on the species—for an agave to bloom, but that's the end of the line. There's no stopping the plant from flowering and subsequently dying, so you might as well enjoy the show.

Agave flower stalks are of two kinds: unbranched with blooms along the stalk (such as *Agave attenuata*) and branching with clusters of flowers (typical of *A. americana*). Regardless, stalks are impressively tall relative to the plants. Thousands of nectar-rich flowers attract hummingbirds, bees, and other pollinators. In some species, flowers form seedpods; in others, they become bulbils that are clones of the mother plant. When the dying mother agave can no longer support its towering stalk, it topples, efficiently propelling seeds or offspring to earth. Start them in nursery flats or small pots until they double in size, and then transplant into larger pots or the garden.

Large agaves produce bloom spikes as tall as sailboat masts. These *Agave franzosinii* are about 7 feet tall; their stalks, three or four times as high.

Harvest thumb-size bulbils along an agave's bloom stalk when they have several leaves and look like miniatures of the mother plant. I chopped this octopus agave's spike at its base to make plantlets easy to access.

Beheading

Leggy aeoniums and showy hybrid echeverias—those that resemble ruffled cabbages—are best propagated by having their "heads" cut off. This sounds drastic, but it's easy to do and rewarding. As the plant grows, its stem elongates, which is not as attractive as a tight rosette with no stem showing. When you tire of looking at the ungainly stem, remove any shriveled leaves from the base of the rosette. With a sharp knife, slice horizontally through the stem, severing the rosette about an inch below the lowest leaves. Place the rosette in a sheltered, shady area, ideally upright with its bottom leaves resting atop an empty pot. In a couple of weeks, the cut end will have callused and sprouted roots. Repot in fresh soil.

Don't discard the original plant's decapitated stem. Keep it in its pot and tend it as when it was intact. New rosettes may grow from one or more leaf axils. When these are 2 to 3 inches in diameter, remove and plant them.

Care and Feeding of Container Succulents

Every nursery, collector, and grower has a preferred container soil mix, which usually includes crushed volcanic rock or perlite; humus-rich soil or compost; and sharp sand, turkey grit, or decomposed granite. Mine is a half-and-half mix of bagged potting soil and pumice, which aerates the soil, provides micronutrients, and absorbs excess water. Some growers prefer perlite, which is lighter in weight, but it is inorganic and nonabsorbent, and it floats. If rainfall, humidity, or cool temperatures tend to keep the soil in pots too moist, add more pumice to the mix.

It's an unfortunate misconception that a layer of gravel in the bottom of a nondraining pot will help drainage. Roots subjected to the resulting microbial soup are actually more prone to rot. For the same reason,

TOP Expert Marylyn Henderson beheads a ruffled echeveria.

BOTTOM A beheaded echeveria has sprouted roots and is ready to be planted.

Succulents in a nondraining container will be fine for years if watered very little.

don't use pot saucers, and beware of containers with bottoms that are slightly convex—water will collect in areas lower than the drain hole.

If a pot has no hole, drill one, or water the plants so minimally that water doesn't pool—about an ounce per plant once or twice a month. The goal is to moisten the roots without saturating the soil. To do this efficiently and to avoid disturbing a decorative topdressing, insert a water-filled syringe into the soil at the base of each plant. Glass containers are easy to monitor, since you can see if the soil is adequately moist (darker in color), and where the water you've added has gone.

Succulents tolerate underwatering because they live on moisture stored in their leaves and stems (as they would in their native habitats). Watering minimally also slows their growth. Consequently, succulents in nondraining containers need repotting less often than their counterparts in pots that drain.

When watering pots with drain holes, do so thoroughly to flush salts that have built up in the soil. In many areas, including southern California, adding a little vinegar to the water (1 tablespoon per gallon) acidifies the soil, which enables roots to more efficiently absorb nutrients. If water pools atop the soil, this indicates that drain holes are plugged, usually from setting pots on bare dirt in the garden. Move them to hardscape or elevate them to allow greater air circulation and discourage ants, slugs, and other pests from entering. Elevation also enhances aesthetics. Place small pots (6 inches in diameter or less) atop repurposed trivets or candle holders and large pots atop pedestals, wrought iron stands, or terra-cotta feet sold at garden centers.

Factors that determine when, how much, and how often to water potted succulents include the weather, the time of year, the type of plant, the size of the pot, the soil consistency, and the pot's location and sun exposure. When humidity is low, temperatures high, and precipitation nonexistent, most potted succulents appreciate a thorough drenching once a week. Note, though, that the smaller the container, the less soil it holds and the more quickly it'll dry out, especially where summers are hot and dry. If it's in full sun, a daily soaking may be in order. But if the same succulent is in dappled shade, humidity is high, and the potting soil is water retentive (having a high percentage of peat moss), weekly watering would likely be excessive.

One way to check soil moisture in pots is to insert a wooden chopstick to a depth of several inches. If the stick feels damp when it's removed, the plant doesn't need water. Any pot exposed to rainfall will not require supplemental water and may need to be moved beneath an overhang to prevent overwatering. On the other hand, letting succulents go dry for too long will cause leaves to lose their sheen, roots to desiccate, and growth to cease. In-ground succulents are not as vulnerable to underwatering as potted ones, because they can send roots deeper and farther to find moisture.

Succulents with dark, glossy leaves may become spotted as water evaporates and minerals accumulate—particularly noticeable with *Aeonium* 'Zwartkop' and *Echeveria agavoides* 'Black Prince'. If you find the white blotches unsightly, remove them by gently wiping the leaves with a soft cloth soaked in distilled water.

Most succulents benefit from repotting every two or three years, but a lot depends on a plant's variety and growth habit. Rosette succulents, for example, may need to be cut back and replanted after a year; small cacti and living stones may be fine in the same pot for five to ten years.

Take care when removing a succulent from its container lest you break the crown and sever the plant from its roots. If it's firmly lodged in a plastic nursery pot, squeeze the container to loosen the soil. If the plant's still stuck, turn the whole thing upside down and cradle the plant as you gently tap the edge of the pot on a solid surface (such as a countertop) to jar the root-ball loose. Or push it up from the bottom with a pencil through the drain hole. If all else fails, cut the plastic and peel it away. Before repotting, gently separate the roots, prune any that are broken or coiled, and check for pests.

With the possible exception of sansevierias, succulents grown as houseplants require bright light for best color and form. Ideal locations are a sunporch, beneath a skylight, or near a window. To prevent leaves from being burned by ultraviolet rays magnified by window glass, place pots a few feet away from the window or cover the glass with a sheer curtain or translucent blind. To prevent etiolation (stems lengthening and becoming spindly), rotate the plants once a week or so for even growth.

A pot stand's birdlike feet repeat the pointed leaves of a dwarf aloe hybrid.

Succulents A to Z

For your designing pleasure, here is an A-to-Z list of my favorite foolproof succulents for gardens large and small. Included are rosette varieties, trees, ground covers, vines, and shrubs. Most are frost tender and winter dormant, and their primary growth period is spring. (If otherwise, that fact is noted.) In addition to descriptions, photos, and cultivation requirements, I share tips and insights based on having grown them in my own garden or observing them in others'.

If you live in a desert climate, pay particular attention to the entries for agaves, cacti, dasylirions, hesperaloes, *Portulacaria afra*, and yuccas; in a northern climate, to those describing sedums (stonecrops) and sempervivums (hens and chicks). No matter where you live, all succulents can be grown in containers, at least when young, provided you give them the proper growing conditions.

All of these are readily available (or becoming so) as there are more succulent sources, both online and brick-and-mortar, than ever before. Shipping succulents smaller than basketballs is commonplace. Expedited delivery is best, and some sources won't ship during midsummer or winter because the plants might cook or freeze in transit. Obtaining large specimens generally means driving to the source—possibly in a rented truck—and transporting the plant yourself or hiring someone to do so. A professional landscape designer or installer can arrange this for you and also purchase the plants at a discount.

Make sure the source has not poached the plants from their native habitats—an unfortunately common occurrence. When in doubt, check with helpful experts at the Cactus and Succulent Society of America (cssainc.org). Among the nonprofit organization's goals is ensuring that these wonderful plants will be protected and enjoyed for generations to come.

A showcase for succulents large and small

When Jeanne Meadow retired from corporate management several years ago, she wanted nothing so much as an inviting garden, provided it needed little water. She researched plants that would look good and also be practical in Fallbrook, California, where temperatures range from the mid-20s F in winter to the high 90s F in summer.

Over the ensuing two years, with the help of north San Diego designer Steve McDearmon of Garden Rhythms, Jeanne created an inviting half-acre gallery of sculptural succulents from South Africa, cacti from the desert Southwest, and echeverias from Mexico. Numerous plants with bold shapes and colors include jades with bright yellow leaves, red paddle plants (*Kalanchoe luciae*), and all sizes of aloes and agaves. Broad paved pathways flow around garden beds that incorporate boulders, crushed rock, and fine gravel. In raised planters just steps from the kitchen, Jeanne grows mint, tomatoes, and other seasonal produce.

Her husband, Barry, says the garden has helped his "high-powered, business-type" wife discover her creativity. "Jeanne studies her collection of succulent books and has visited every succulent grower within 50 miles." She also joined the Cactus and Succulent Society of America and conducts occasional workshops on container gardening with succulents. "I can't get enough of them," she says.

Jeanne Meadow's garden is mainly succulents but also has raised beds for edibles. Brazilian pepper trees provide shade and a lacy texture.

ABOVE In a large pot between driveway and entry, Jeanne planted *Aeonium* 'Zwartkop' for height, *Aloe dorotheae* as a textural filler, and the dwarf, prostrate form of *Portulacaria afra* (sometimes called 'Minima') as a cascader.

ABOVE, RIGHT An agave's bloom spike is impressive but unfortunately announces the end of the plant's life cycle. Also in bloom are echeverias, aloes, and *Crassula pubescens*. At center foreground, with fingerlike leaves, is *Cotyledon orbiculata* var. *oblonga* 'Flavida'.

Agave "Blue Glow" (upper left) stands out against yellow *Sedum adolphi* (foreground, right) and mounding shrub crassulas. Alongside the boulder at lower left is a dark purple dyckia.

Agave salmiana, one of the largest agaves, is the focal point of a garden bed that includes aloes in bloom, *Euphorbia milii* (red flowers at lower left), and at center, *Aeonium* 'Zwartkop', 'Sunset' jade, and fan-shaped *Aloe plicatilis*.

Aeonium 'Sunburst' and A. arboreum

Aeonium 'Kiwi' and A. haworthii blend at lower right. Nearby are larger A. canariense rosettes (note the one left of center elongating into bloom), blue Senecio mandraliscae, jade, and with orange flowers, Aloe striata.

Aeonium

Aeoniums, the majority of which resemble green daisies with glossy, overlapping leaves, vary from single-trunked rosettes to branching shrubs. Most rosettes are smooth and shiny, but every so often you'll run across a variety with a delicately furred texture due to nearly invisible, short, translucent hairs—a delightful surprise. When an aeonium blooms, the entire rosette elongates into a conical inflorescence massed with dime-size cream, yellow, or pink flowers. Each rosette dies after blooming, but this has little impact on plants with many, because not all rosettes bloom at once.

Because they are native to the Canary Islands and Morocco, aeoniums thrive outdoors in zone 9 (and higher if in dappled shade). Most species are summer dormant, so their growth season is winter. Water them in summer only enough to keep the roots from desiccating. Most aeoniums will survive temps down to the mid-20s F if covered with frost cloth or bedsheets. They're common in gardens that have dry summers, winter rain, low humidity, and a mild climate (such as the California coast), but aeoniums are seldom seen where humidity is high and rain falls in summer (such as Hawaii and Florida). Nor do they do well as indoor houseplants. In such conditions aeoniums are prone to mealybug infestations, fungus diseases, and root rot.

So-called black aeoniums (*Aeonium* 'Zwartkop' and its hybrids) are actually a deep burgundy, a color evident when sun backlights the leaves. When the plants are grown in too little light, the centers turn green. In the garden, such inky plants disappear, so position them in front of light-colored shrubs, walls, fences, or boulders.

In mild climates, late fall and early winter are the best times to prune and replant a bed of lanky aeoniums—typical of *Aeonium arboreum* (the species name means trunk forming) and its selections. Cut the rosettes, leaving several inches of stem, and discard the rest of the plant, roots and all. (Roots are seldom deeper than 3 inches.) If the remaining soil is compacted, add amendments such as compost and pumice to enhance its friability, enabling cuttings to root easily. Replant the rosettes, using each one's stub of trunk to anchor it. By spring the cuttings will have rooted and the rosettes will be a glorious bed of glossy pinwheels.

Aeonium 'Jack Catlin' rosettes have chartreuse centers and berry-toned tips. As they grow and crowd each other, they form a multihued mass.

Although its origin is uncertain, *Aeonium* 'Kiwi' is likely a hybrid of gray-green *A. haworthii*. The two have a similar shrub-forming growth habit, rosette size, and red-margined edges. The more sun they get, the lighter *Aeonium* 'Kiwi' leaves will be. Take care, however, not to let the plant sunburn.

Aeonium flowers (like those of *Aeonium* 'Zwartkop' shown here), which form in spring, can be picked for long-stemmed bouquets. They need no water, and buds continue to open for weeks.

Aeonium 'Jack Catlin'

Teeth and spines of *Agave potatorum* create bud imprints.

Agave

The statuesque, fountainlike forms of large agaves lend a sculptural element to any landscape and relieve the textural monotony of finer-leaved plants. Large agaves also make good firebreak plants and security fences. Those smaller than basketballs are excellent potted plants. Display small agaves—there are many exquisite ones—one to a pot. Agaves with long, serpentine terminal spines and prominent teeth along the margins are both graceful and fierce, like a cat that yawns and shows its fangs. Scalloped patterns on an agave's leaves ("bud imprints") are caused by spines and teeth pressing into the flesh of inner leaves before they unfurl.

Sharp points at leaf tips and along leaf edges make agaves treacherous to weed around. Snip a quarter inch from the tips with garden shears to protect yourself and others from impalement. When pruning an agave, trim the leaf to a "V" that resembles its natural tip, or cut it back all the way to the trunk. (A straight-across cut at a leaf's midsection ruins the plant's symmetry.) Avoid getting sap on your skin as it may cause an allergic reaction.

With the exception of a few soft-leaved and variegated varieties, agaves want sun—the more the better in all but desert climes. Most are hardy to the mid- to high 20s F, and some go a lot lower. If an agave is exceptionally frost tender or cold hardy, it's noted here. Agaves propagate by blooming, and some also produce pups by way of shallow rhizomes (lateral roots). Being indigenous to the New World (the American Southwest, Mexico, and Central America), larger agaves store enough moisture to get by on rainfall alone and will thrive in nutrient-poor soils. Large agaves that pup are the thugs of the plant world; they'll grow and spread rapidly when given good soil and regular irrigation. Such pampering isn't necessary and may lead to early flowering—not a good thing. Although agaves like water, their roots—like those of most succulents—will rot in waterlogged soil.

All but a few agaves are monocarpic, meaning they bloom once and then die. This may take as many as twenty-five years, but it *will* happen. As it completes its life cycle, a mature rosette that has graced a garden

Notice the abundant offsets (pups) surrounding these specimens of *Agave americana*.

White-striped *Agave americana* 'Mediopicta Alba', green *A. salmiana*, blue *A. franzosinii* (two of the largest species), ground-covering *Senecio mandraliscae*, and blazing *Euphorbia tirucalli* 'Sticks on Fire' grace a mounded front-yard garden.

for years sends up an asparagus-like flower stalk (most, but not all, branch). This dwarfs the plant and saps its energy. Flowers along the stalk eventually turn into miniplants (bulbils) or seed capsules. Only the flowering rosette dies; in many cases—notably with those involving *Agave americana*—a litter of pups will carry on.

Agave americana (10 to 15 feet tall and wide) is commonly called century plant because it seems to take a century to bloom (though it actually flowers at fifteen to twenty-five years of age). The plant's long, tapered, blue-green leaves are 6 to 10 inches wide, grow to 6 to 8 feet long, and are rigid and leathery, with hooked prickles along the edges and sharp-pointed tips. Pups enlarge the plants' domain indefinitely.

Even small century plants thrive with no care at all. Like cactus, they don't mind frost, blazing sun, or poor soil. Plant on rocky slopes where nothing else will grow and in any large area that receives little or no irrigation.

I used to advise people not to grow americanas in containers because the roots are pot breakers. Now, because pups can be invasive, I suggest growing americanas *only* in large, sturdy pots. There are pros and cons to both—indeed, to growing americanas at all. These most majestic of agaves are free for the asking; a neighbor who has one will gladly hand you a shovel. However,

later on, you'll have to remove the same plant's mutts, unless you don't mind donating costly real estate to an ever-expanding colony, not to mention losing the statuesque symmetry that attracted you to the mother ship in the first place. Because of this undesirable trait, hybridizers are working on *Agave* cultivars that offset infrequently, if at all.

Variegated selections of *Agave americana* include 'Marginata' (to 8 feet tall and wide) and white-striped *A. americana* 'Mediopicta Alba' (tuxedo agave), 3 to 4 feet tall and wide. These and closely related, light blue *A. franzosinii* share many traits with the blue-gray species but are more sensitive to frost and intense sun. All pup like undomesticated dogs.

Agave angustifolia 'Marginata' (4 feet tall and wide) has long green-and-cream striped, tapered leaves that give the plant a starburst shape. It's cold hardy to around 20°F and forms tight colonies.

Agave attenuata (to 5 feet tall and wide) is common in gardens along the California coast and in Florida and Hawaii; elsewhere it needs protection from frost and sunburn. It is an anomaly among agaves in that it is trunk forming. Offsets that grow along the trunk eventually form a dense cluster. Smooth, flexible leaves have no vicious barbs and lack terminal spines, and the flower

Agave 'Baccarat'

Agave americana 'Marginata'

Agave attenuata 'Variegata'

ABOVE In Patrick Anderson's garden, multiples of *Agave angustifolia* 'Marginata' stand out amid cactus, aloes, and the feathery leaves of a pepper tree.

spike is tall, arching, and unbranched, hence the common name foxtail agave. Blue varieties exist but are uncommon. Variegates of *A. attenuata* are striped or streaked with yellow or cream, seldom offset, and may sunburn if unprotected.

Agave 'Baccarat' (crystal bowl agave) grows to 4 feet tall and wide and is solitary (doesn't produce offsets). Leaves are concave isosceles triangles with long terminal spines, teal blue with a rosy blush and patterned with white bud imprints. Native to the high mountains of Mexico, it is one of the more cold-tolerant agaves—to 0°F. Protect from intense sun lest leaves scorch.

Agave 'Blue Flame' (to 4 feet tall and wide) has broad, flexible blue-green leaves that suggest the flames of a gas burner and have finely serrated edges. Long, needlelike tips turn inward, making them less hazardous than if they curved outward. Forms offsets.

One of the most popular landscape succulents, *Agave* 'Blue Glow', should have been named 'Red Glow'

Agave 'Blue Flame' (top) and A. 'Blue Glow' (below)

Smooth-leaved *Agave bracteosa* contrasts with a crested cactus and yellow sedum.

because its leaves—with painterly striations of green, blue, and gray—have translucent red margins. It's an excellent medium-sized agave (to 3 feet in diameter) with a crisp silhouette of slender, tapered leaves. Doesn't produce pups.

Agave bracteosa (green spider agave) has long, narrow, tapered, bright green leaves that curl downward and lack spines. Center leaves that cling to each other have outward-pointing tips that give the plant a distinctive star-shaped center. Although it looks delicate, this is one of the more cold-hardy agaves (to 10°F). Wiggle loose any offsets so the mother plant retains her svelte silhouette. Grows well in bright or dappled shade.

Agave lophantha 'Quadricolor', a prolific pupper, orchestrated this arrangement on its own.

Accompanying a pair of *Agave desmetiana* 'Variegata' plants in bloom are blue *Senecio mandraliscae*, *Aeonium* 'Kiwi', purple statice, and variegated furcraeas.

Agave ovatifolia

Agave desmetiana 'Variegata' (3 feet tall and 3 feet wide) has upright, gracefully curved leaves margined in yellow. It blooms (and therefore dies) early compared to other agaves, around five years of age.

Agave lophantha 'Quadricolor', a visually dynamic variegate of a tough and hardy desert agave, stays small (mature rosettes to 12 inches in diameter) and provides the look of yellow-and-green-striped starbursts in garden beds. Place it where its numerous offspring are welcome.

Several species of agave have white, curly filaments along the leaf margins that may strike you as messy, lovely, or intriguing—perhaps all three. These translucent white threads soften the look of stiff and spiky plants, adding contrast in form as well as attitude. Filamented agaves are eye catching when backlit. *Agave*

multifilifera stays small (1 to 2 feet) and is best displayed in a container.

Agave ovatifolia somewhat resembles *A. parryi* var. *truncata*, which also has broad, rounded leaves, but *A. ovatifolia* is larger, light blue, and generally more showy; perhaps most important, it doesn't pup. Hardy to 5°F or lower, it attains 6 feet in diameter.

Agave parryi (Parry's agave) is gray with black serrated edges and long black tips. Native to the desert Southwest and Mexico, it is highly heat tolerant yet also among the most cold hardy of agaves, to –20°F. Plants seldom grow larger than 2 feet tall and wide. *Agave parryi* var. *truncata* has broad, oval leaves, grows to 4 feet in diameter, and is much less cold tolerant than the species (to 15°F). It's beautiful grown in multiples, and since it tends to offset, that's likely to happen.

Agave multifilifera

Agave parryi in a Texas garden

Agave parryi var. truncata

Agave 'Sharkskin'

Agave salmiana 'Green Giant'

Agave shawii

Use *Agave salmiana* to repeat the shapes of other succulent behemoths, such as the americanas, or solo as a garden focal point. Grows to 6 feet tall and 12 feet in diameter over time. Stiff leaves curve up and out, reminiscent of a multi-armed Hindu deity. Plant where pups won't cause problems, perhaps in a stone terrace.

Agave 'Sharkskin', a medium-size (2 to 3 feet in diameter) agave, is a tough plant in the garden and a wonderful conversation piece. Leaves have the texture of fine sandpaper and are so thick and inflexible they might be made of plywood. Hardy to the mid-20s F.

When backlit, the toothed edges of *Agave shawii* glow pink, orange, yellow, and red. Native to Baja California, *Agave shawii* handles drought and poor soil like a champ, grows slowly, and produces offsets from stems

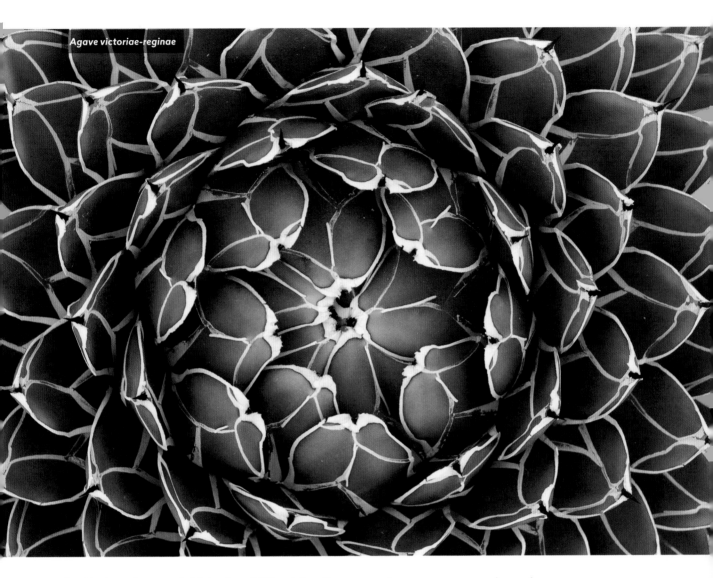

Agave victoriae-reginae

that lie along the ground. It's hardy to 25°F and does fine in desert gardens if given afternoon shade.

Agave victoriae-reginae (Queen Victoria agave) has a tight, artichoke-like symmetry and leaves detailed with white lines. It grows to 12 inches tall by 18 inches wide, is cold hardy to 10°F, and seldom produces offsets. It's famous for taking its time to bloom—twenty years or so. Although the tall, skinny bloom spike is nothing much to look at, one feels compelled not to ignore such a momentous event. Closely related to *A. victoriae-reginae* is *A. nickelsiae* (formerly *A. ferdinandi-regis*), which has longer gray-green leaves, white lines that appear drawn with chalk, and squiggly black tips.

Agave vilmoriniana (5 feet tall and wide) has narrow, guttered, blue-green leaves that undulate as though swept by an ocean current—hence the common name octopus agave. Because leaf edges lack teeth, it's considered a "soft" agave. The species is solitary, but plantlets do form abundantly along the bloom spike. Hardy to the low 20s F; sensitive to overwatering. The yellow-striped variegate is *A. vilmoriniana* 'Stained Glass'.

With its minimally serrated margins and graceful, tapered leaves, *Agave weberi* epitomizes agave elegance. It's better behaved (less inclined to offset) than the americanas it resembles but is slightly more sensitive to weather extremes (hardy to 25°F; needs afternoon shade in the heat of summer). Grows to 6 feet tall and up to 10 feet wide.

Agave nickelsiae

Agave weberi 'Arizona Star'

Repeating the upward-arching leaves of a pair of *Agave vilmoriniana* 'Stained Glass' in this Pismo Beach, California, front yard is *Aloe vanbalenii* (lower left). At center foreground is another variegate: *Kalanchoe luciae* 'Fantastic'.

Aloes and agaves: Important differences

Newcomers to the world of succulents sometimes have difficulty determining if a plant is an aloe or an agave. Both form rosettes of tapered green or gray-blue leaves that spiral up and outward from the base. Certain members of both genera also produce offsets from their roots.

Aloes bloom year after year, but with few exceptions, after an agave flowers, it dies. Agaves are useful primarily for the symmetry of their foliage, though bloom spikes are indeed impressive and on large specimens may last several months. This tendency to look lovely for a decade and then die rather suddenly is a drawback to growing agaves; another is that most have thorny leaf margins and needlelike tips.

To identify a mystery plant, first examine teeth along the leaves. Not all agaves and aloes have prickles and barbs, but when they do, agaves have them only along leaf edges, and each leaf ends in a hard point. Prickles on aloes not only line leaf margins but also may appear elsewhere. Barbs on agaves are of denser tissue (like fingernail or horn) than that of the leaves, and there's a clear delineation between the two. Prickles on aloes appear to have been pulled, taffylike, from the leaf surface. The teeth of aloes, being softer than those of agaves, are less likely to pierce the skin of an unfortunate passerby.

Other differences not immediately apparent are that agaves have fibrous leaves; those of aloes are filled with thick gel—which to horticulturists is the key determinant. Agave leaves are stiffer than those of aloes that have comparable thickness and are less prone to breaking or snapping off. Aloes come from Africa and Madagascar; agaves from the Americas. In fact, agaves were initially referred to as New World aloes.

BOTTOM LEFT *Agave titanota* has toothed leaf margins and stiff terminal spines. Leaves are firmer and tougher than those of similarly shaped aloes.

BOTTOM RIGHT Light-colored prickles on this *Aloe* ×*nobilis* 'Variegata' consist of the same tissue as the leaves.

Is it an aloe or an agave? At first glance, sharp-looking protrusions along the leaf margins suggest an agave, but look again: they're also along each leaf's keel (center back). Plump leaves indicate juiciness, and prickles (though different in color) are the same tissue as the leaf. This is *Aloe erinacea* from Namibia.

Aloe brevifolia

Aloe

Aloes range in size from small plants 2 to 4 inches in diameter to trees 20 feet tall or more. Some are solitary and trunk forming, while others offset into ever-expanding colonies. The majority produce flowers in midwinter, but there's at least one species in bloom at any time of the year. Flower spikes consist of tubular blossoms in shades of orange, red, or yellow (and occasionally cream, pink, green, or bicolor). Most aloes cannot handle a hard freeze, and the leaves of many species redden when the plant is stressed by cold, drought, or more sun and less rich soil than it prefers.

Native to southern and eastern Africa, the Arabian Peninsula, and Madagascar, aloes do best when watered regularly year-round—on average every two weeks while actively growing in spring and summer, less in fall, and not at all in winter. Those sensitive to summer watering are not included here.

Give aloes as much light as possible, short of desert sun, to encourage flowering and to maintain the red and orange hues in their leaves. Although the ideal temperature range for aloes is 40 to 90°F, most can handle temperatures from 25 to 100°F for short periods. If a species or cultivar is less or more cold or heat tolerant than the norm, it's noted here.

The old foliage of many aloes curves downward, dries, and clings to the stem. If you find this unsightly, remove the dead leaves. However, keep in mind they exist to protect the aloe's stem or trunk from cold, heat, and sunburn. Moreover, when they shade the ground beneath the plant, the soil doesn't dry out as quickly, so they benefit the roots as well.

Diminutive *Aloe* cultivars good for container and rock gardens have teacup-size rosettes. The slender, spaghetti-like bloom spikes of these small aloes are insignificant—although hummingbirds appreciate them, as they do all aloe flowers.

Aloe arborescens (torch aloe) forms multiheaded mounds of 1-to-3-foot-diameter rosettes. It's often found in frost-free coastal gardens in southern California, unperturbed by nutrient-poor, sandy soil and salt spray. Tight clusters of serrated green leaves overlap like sea stars clinging to a rock. Over time, a colony can grow to 6 feet tall and twice as wide. In midwinter, *A. arborescens* sends up torchlike spires of red-orange flowers. A

LEFT 'Christmas Carol' is one of many dwarf aloe cultivars created by hybridizer Kelly Griffin.

BOTTOM *Aloe barberae* in a front-yard garden is underplanted with smaller aloes and other succulents, among them blue *Senecio mandraliscae*.

Aloe arborescens

yellow-streaked variegate, which needs protection from sun-scorch and frost, grows well in bright shade but like most aloes isn't likely to bloom without sun.

Stiff, downward-curving leaves make *Aloe barberae* (also sold as *A. bainesii*) resemble the trees in books by children's author Dr. Seuss. Young specimens, 3 to 4 feet tall in 15-gallon pots, tend to be single-headed (unbranched) until they reach 5 or 6 feet tall. Eventually they attain 20 feet in height. Leaves are prone to get black spots, especially in cool, foggy maritime climates; a similar-looking, more disease-resistant alternative is 'Hercules', a hybrid of *A. barberae* and *A. dichotoma*.

Two tough aloes look alike due to their similar size, shape, and hen-and-chicks growth habit: blue-green *Aloe brevifolia* (short-leaf aloe) and bright green *A.* ×*nobilis* (gold tooth aloe). Both form ever-expanding, tightly packed colonies of rosettes that eventually attain 10 to 12 inches in diameter. In summer, plants send up slender orange spires. Both species also survive frost and near-desert heat, aren't fussy about soil, grow in dappled or full sun, tolerate too little or too much water, and turn lovely colors when stressed.

Aloe ×nobilis reddens with sun exposure.

Among the most sought-after aloes for its color is *Aloe cameronii*, which has foot-long tapered, serrated green leaves that turn cranberry red when the plant is grown in full sun. Overlapping rosettes form clusters several feet high and wide.

Aloe camperi, an especially floriferous aloe, forms an ever-expanding colony of offsets. In May, it's massed with 3-foot-tall orange flowers.

Aloe dorotheae, prized for both its salmon red color (when stressed) and its compact form, has 12-inch-diameter rosettes that resemble stacked sea stars. Blooming is hardly necessary, but it does that, too.

Aloe ferox (6 to 10 feet tall) forms a single trunk with a crown of 3-to-4-foot toothed leaves that are smooth or minimally prickled. Columnar spikes of

red- or yellow-orange flowers rise several feet above the center of the plant in midwinter.

Thanks to its light blue color, small size (6 inches wide by 8 inches tall), and numerous white prickles suggesting polka dots, *Aloe humilis* is a great little plant for potted combos.

Aloe maculata (also sold as *A. saponaria*) is commonly called soap aloe; supposedly, the sap produces suds in water. Triangular speckled or banded leaves are reddish green and short when grown in strong sun, dark green and elongated in partial shade. Growing 6 to 8 inches high and 6 to 12 inches wide, *A. maculata* produces tall (to 2½ feet) branching stems in late spring massed with panicles of tubular orange flowers. (They're not good in bouquets—too gooey.) *Aloe maculata* offsets

Orange- and red-flowering varieties of *Aloe cameronii* bloom in January in Hannah Jarson's garden.

Aloe ferox at peak bloom in mid-January towers over a blue form of *Agave attenuata*; the cactus alongside it is *Cereus repandus*.

Aloe camperi

Aloe dorotheae

Aloe humilis with *Echeveria* 'Perle von Nürnberg'

Flowering *Aloe maculata* with A. ×*nobilis* and red-leaved *Kalanchoe luciae* behind it

In a Texas garden, *Aloe vera* benefits from a sun-warmed wall.

freely and can be invasive in friable (soft) soils. Like other plants that get unruly in a well-tended garden, this weed of an aloe works well in areas where few other plants thrive.

Aloe marlothii (to 8 feet tall), like *A. ferox*, is trunk forming and produces vivid, Popsicle-like flowers in winter. Similar in size, the two species are often confused, but *A. marlothii* blooms several months later (in spring), flower stems branch horizontally, and leaves are prickled—sometimes heavily so.

Aloe polyphylla (spiral aloe), with triangular blue-green leaves that form a tight, symmetrical whorl, is native to the high mountains of Lesotho, South Africa, and is in danger of extinction in the wild. Spiral aloes don't mind being buried beneath snow provided they have exceptionally well-drained soil. Although *A. polyphylla* may never be common in hot, dry Southwest succulent gardens, it does fine in cooler, wetter northern California. Avoid supplemental water in winter because the plants are susceptible to fusarium, a fungus that causes rot. Look for spiral aloes grown from seed; those that are tissue cultured (that is, clones) tend to have a less compact form.

Aloe speciosa, with multiheaded clusters to 6 feet tall and wide, produces spectacular conical flowers banded with cream, pink, and rose-red blossoms fringed with rust-orange stamens. It's commonly called tilt-head aloe because the large leaf rosettes lean in the direction of greatest sun.

Aloe striata (2 feet tall and wide), known as coral aloe, has stemless gray-green leaves subtly striped and tinged with orange, lavender, and rose. Translucent, 1/8-inch-wide leaf margins are edged with coral and lack teeth (although a hybrid common in cultivation does have them).

Aloe vanbalenii has curved, overlapping chartreuse leaves that turn bright orange when stressed. Plants form mounds that can attain several feet in height and diameter.

Aloe vera (formerly *A. barbadensis*), to 3 feet tall, is famous for gel in the leaves that soothes minor burns and other skin irritations. Leaves are gray-green and upright; bloom stalks, tall and slender with yellow flowers.

Aloe marlothii is at peak bloom in April in a San Luis Obispo, California, garden.

Aloe polyphylla

Aloe speciosa

Aloe vanbalenii with A. 'Hercules' at upper left

Aloe striata

ABOVE *Beaucarnea stricta*

ABOVE, RIGHT *Beaucarnea recurvata* in bloom. The plants are either male (with straw-colored flowers) or female (pink, as pictured here).

Beaucarnea

A young beaucarnea has the look of a feather duster anchored by a suction cup. Like other succulents with nonfleshy foliage, beaucarneas have a caudex (an enlarged, woody base) that stores water like a camel's hump. The trees grow to 20+ feet tall with bulbous bases that may expand to 8 or more feet in diameter. *Beaucarnea recurvata* has downward-curving leaves and a fissured caudex; *B. stricta* has straight, stiff leaves resembling those of a yucca, and a caudex textured like a tortoise's shell. Despite the common names bottle palm and ponytail palm, the genus is not related to palms.

Beaucarneas are intriguing when grouped and effective solo as garden exclamation points. The plants can go dry for long periods and are sensitive to overwatering. Provide porous soil with excellent drainage and water sparingly in winter lest stems rot. Young specimens do well in pots.

Bulbine frutescens 'Hallmark' adds vertical interest to a mounded arrangement that includes sedums, echeverias, pachyverias, sempervivums, and trailing *Senecio rowleyanus* (string of pearls).

Young cardons (*Pachycereus pringlei*) glow in late afternoon sun.

Bulbine

Bulbine frutescens (18-inch leaves, with flower stems of 2 to 3 feet) has juicy, pencil-thick leaves that are pointed at the tips. Airy sprays of tiny yellow or orange flowers top skinny stems. Plants are effective when massed, are unfussy about soil, and grow in semishade to full sun.

Cactus

Cacti are truly remarkable. They bake in desert sun without shriveling, remain moist on the inside despite months without rain, and if edible manage not to be eaten.

Ribbed cacti contract when no water is available, creating furrows that expose less surface area to the sun. Roots are shallow and needed mainly for rehydration, and because they regenerate rapidly, enable cuttings or offsets to establish quickly. Vivid, satiny flowers attract pollinators from miles away.

Spines are modified leaves that fend off thirsty predators and shade the plants' skin. They may be flat, conical, daggerlike, papery, stiff, flexible, rigid, soft, hooked, barbed, or curved. Such weaponry is the reason few gardeners are interested in growing cacti. Yet in terms of aesthetics, I believe that just as an appreciation of foliage over flowers indicates a gardener's growing sophistication, so does an appreciation of spines over leaves. I call certain cacti "halo plants" because of how their spines glow in early morning or late afternoon light. This plus their shapes, textures, and patterns make cacti a joy to collect and to photograph.

All cacti are succulents, but unlike other succulents, cacti have areoles—points that contain meristematic tissue from which spines, pads, flowers, or new branches grow. All cacti—and most succulents—have a thick skin or protective coating that seals in moisture. This may be white and powdery (farinose) or waxy and blue-green

Spines of *Echinocereus rigidissimus* var. *rubispinus* look like embroidery.

Pilosocereus maxonii protects its buds, flowers, and fruit with what looks like cotton.

Cereus hildmannianus

Cereus hildmannianus 'Monstrosus' is in scale with the large boulder behind it. With it are *Euphorbia tirucalli* 'Sticks on Fire', *Agave americana* 'Marginata', yuccas, and lavender in bloom.

(glaucous). Cactus flowers are breathtaking but short lived, lasting just a day or two. Fruits of many cacti are edible, and in some cases (as is true of opuntias) so is the flesh.

Cacti are indigenous to the Americas, from Tierra del Fuego to central Canada, and are found on grassy plains, along the coasts, and in mountains and deserts. Because their skin contains chlorophyll, the plants are able to photosynthesize. They store water in cylindrical, spherical, jointed, or padlike stems. Globular cacti, such as golden barrels, are especially efficient at retaining moisture and minimizing evaporation.

Several kinds of cacti produce what resembles white fur or hair. Such bearding serves as both sunscreen and sweater, begs for anthropomorphic analogies, and is mesmerizing when backlit.

When designing with cacti, keep in mind the three distinct forms most useful in landscaping: columnar cacti that often have "cereus" in their Latin names (ceroids), cacti with jointed stems (paddle cacti and chollas), and globular types from large to small (barrels to pincushions).

Most cacti need no irrigation at all from early to late winter. In spring, water should gradually be increased, and in summer, cacti do best when watered once or twice a week, depending on heat, humidity, and soil porosity.

Soil should be coarse and fast draining and allowed to go dry or nearly so between waterings. Avoid letting water pool at the base of the plant. Irrigate with drip or, if plants are on a steep slope, dig a trench or basin above them and fill it with water. Gravity will send moisture to the roots without getting the crowns of the plants wet. Position new plants with the same orientation to the sun that they had in the nursery, lest they sunburn (mark the pots). Water dormant and newly planted cacti very little or not at all. Wait several weeks after planting to give broken roots a chance to heal.

Unless otherwise noted, all cacti included here tolerate temperatures from the mid-20s to 105°F. When frost threatens, cover the growing tips of columnar cactus; Styrofoam cups turned upside down will work, but little Santa hats have more panache.

Cereus hildmannianus (long known as *C. peruvianus*), the most commonly cultivated ceroid species, is native to South America. Columnar trunks grow to 15 feet tall and about 12 inches in diameter. These produce vertical branches that eventually form 10-foot-wide trees. Each branch has ribs bearing stiff gray spines. Large, fragrant, creamy white flowers emerge at night in summer, followed by edible red fruit. A popular monstrose form's knobby columns resemble melted wax.

Cleistocactus strausii

Textures, shapes, and colors repeat and contrast in a garden that includes silver torch cactus, golden barrels, blue senecios, red *Kalanchoe luciae*, a dasylirion, red-flowered *Euphorbia milii*, a blue agave, graptoverias, and blue baseball bat cactus (*Pilosocereus pachycladus*).

Cleistocactus strausii (silver torch cactus), to 8 feet tall, is columnar and densely covered with fine white hairlike spines. Position it where early morning or late afternoon sun will halo the plant.

Echinocactus grusonii (golden barrel cactus), to 3 feet in diameter, is a ribbed sphere covered with down-ward-curving, butter-yellow spines. Plant them en masse or in random groupings—where they appear to roll across the landscape—or solo in circular pots. As they age, golden barrels produce offsets that cling to the sides of the mother plant. Yellow flowers crown mature specimens in summer. Plants can handle drought, frost, full sun, and desert heat—everything except excessive moisture.

Ferocactus literally means fierce cactus. These ribbed, stout-spined cacti from Mexico and the Southwest are spherical when young. Many varieties become cylindrical with age. Some are solitary, while others eventually form clumps. Common in cultivation is *F. latispinus*, which has red spines that glow fire-bright in slanted sunlight.

Mammillaria is a large genus with more than a hundred species. Most are spherical, at least when young, and they often form colonies that resemble spiny stacked balls. Use them to fill bowl-shaped pots and as appealing accents in rock gardens.

Opuntia or prickly pear is the most wide-ranging genus of cacti, occurring from Argentina all the way to Canada. Plants have large satiny blooms and pad-dle-shaped or cylindrical stems linked one to another. In

Echinocactus grusonii with gaillardia

Ferocactus latispinus

Peter Walkowiak's collection includes many fine old specimens of various *Mammillaria* species, including the clump of white-spined *M. hahniana* at center.

addition to needlelike spines, and sometimes instead of them, most opuntias are armed with nubby, nearly invisible barbed filaments called glochids. These come off the plant easily and are irritating to the skin. How to remove them is a favorite topic among cactus collectors. Most methods involve various kinds of glue or tape being placed on the skin and then peeled away with the hope that the glochid goes with it. I have good luck with duct tape.

The genus *Opuntia* includes succulents I wouldn't have in my garden because they're so treacherous, and those that I wouldn't be without because they're the best-ever plants. Those on my keep-away-from list include *O. microdasys*, due to its abundant glochids; and also anything in the related genus *Cylindropuntia*, known as chollas, since these have vicious spines and cylindrical joints that detach all too easily. (Members of the Tucson Cactus and Succulent Society, please note: after you enlightened me on the joys of chollas, I developed a sincere appreciation for their beauty and usefulness. Even so, I dare not grow them.)

Famed plant hybridizer Luther Burbank (1849–1926) dreamed of making a fortune by developing a spineless opuntia that would serve as cattle feed and provide all the moisture the animals need, and that ranchers would find easier and more economical than grain to grow, harvest, and store. He came up with numerous cultivars, the best known of which is 'Burbank Spineless', but it has been known to regress (grow spines and glochids). In my garden I have a spineless opuntia that the source can't identify; it might be Burbank's 'Avalon' or possibly *Opuntia cacanapa* 'Ellisiana' (to 5°F). In a landscape, smooth paddle cacti offer an unfussy green backdrop that needs no irrigation and is easy to garden around. The fruit and tender young pads, like those of other opuntias, are edible.

The most requested plant in my garden, when it comes to cuttings, is a dwarf, purple-leaved variety of *Opuntia basilaris* (beavertail prickly pear) that produces satiny pink blooms and happens to be remarkably hardy, to −15 or −20°F. *Opuntia santa-rita* (often sold as *O. violacea* var. *santa-rita*), to 4 feet tall and 6 feet wide, has pads that range from green to lavender-pink (the more sun, the better the color).

Pilosocereus means hairy columnar cactus, and the genus comprises fifty or so hirsute succulents from Mexico, Central America, and northern South America. They prefer dry winters and wet summers, so water

A spineless opuntia, possibly *Opuntia cacanapa* 'Ellisiana'

Opuntia basilaris thrives in a garden near Portland, Oregon. Alongside it is comparably cold-hardy *Agave montana*.

In a Tucson garden, *Opuntia santa-rita* contrasts in form and color with the palo verde tree behind it.

The common name, bunny ears, is misleading: *Opuntia microdasys* is thickly dotted with glochids.

accordingly, and protect the growing tips from frost. *Pilosocereus pachycladus* is an amazing azure blue.

Trichocereus (also sold as *Echinopsis*) hybrids are grown mainly for their blooms. For most of the year, the plants are bristly green posts. Come spring, they form horizontal buds that resemble flamingo heads. These explode into masses of large flowers that, depending on the variety, are one of a dozen hot hues or pastel shades of peach, pink, yellow, or white. Collectors plan their vacations around the plants' anticipated flowering and when it happens, host impromptu parties.

Fascinating fasciations

Crested growth (fasciation) is found more in cacti and succulents than in the rest of the plant kingdom. Cresting happens when new growth emerges from a line rather than a point. Some crests look like brains; others, pythons, alluvial fans, coral outcroppings, or stretch waistbands. Cresting is spontaneous and unpredictable, and no two crests are exactly alike. Because such mutants tend to be slow growing, the older the crest, the more prized by collectors.

LEFT *Pilosocereus pachycladus* with red-flowering *Euphorbia milii*

BELOW *Trichocereus* hybrid

Graptopetalum paraguayense, normal (right) and crested (left).

Mammillaria bombycina f. cristata (above) appears happier than its spherical form.

Disocactus flagelliformis

Epiphyllum flower

Crested, or cristate, varieties are identified in a plant's Latin name as *cristata* or *cristatus*. Odd lumpy forms, sometimes but not always caused by cresting, are monstrose, added to the plant's Latin name as *monstrosa* or *monstrosus*. Sometimes a crest is so convoluted or unusual, only an expert can discern what kind of plant it is.

To prevent rot, give a crested or monstrose succulent less water than you would the normal version of the same plant. If there is both crested and normal growth, prune away the latter to direct energy to the crest; otherwise, the more vigorous tissue will take over.

Crests that lack chlorophyll are sold grafted onto a cactus that does have it (referred to as the rootstock). The host plant needs enough sun to photosynthesize, while the crested plant needs sun protection, so such pairings are best grown in bright shade or greenhouse conditions. Grafts must be redone when the crest outgrows its host. Monstrose and crested succulents that grow on their own roots are tougher, and many are readily available and will thrive in mild-climate gardens.

Jungle cacti

Cacti from Central and South American jungles are understory plants sheltered from hot sun by the trees among which they grow. Those common in cultivation include species and cultivars of these genera: *Disocactus*,

Cistanthe grandiflora

Cotyledon tomentosa

also sold as *Aporocactus* (which have fuzzy, snakelike limbs that radiate from a central point); *Epiphyllum*, with long, leaflike, segmented stems and showy flowers (for which they're collected); *Hatiora* (Easter cactus), which bloom in spring; *Hylocereus* (dragonfruit), *Lepismium*, and *Rhipsalis*, which form masses of trailing, jointed stems; and *Schlumbergera* (Christmas cactus), which bloom in December.

Disocactus flagelliformis is commonly called rat-tail cactus for its slender stems, which are several feet long and about an inch in diameter. Though bristly, they are soft to the touch. The cactus is native to Mexico and has red blooms.

Most tropical cacti need humus-rich, well-aerated soil that stays moist, protection from temperatures below 40°F, and enough bright light to bloom but not burn. Typical of cacti in general, flowers are satiny and in warm hues. Except in mild maritime climates where the plants receive morning sun only, they should be cultivated in greenhouses, lath houses, or beneath tree canopies in dappled shade. Being naturally pendant, jungle cacti do best in hanging baskets.

Cistanthe

Cistanthe (formerly *Calandrinia*) is a varied genus encompassing about 150 species of purslane, all of which bear colorful flowers. *Cistanthe grandiflora* forms a low, mounding shrub with gray-green leaves. Plants send up wire-thin, nodding flower spikes several feet tall, topped with clusters of vivid purple, poppylike blooms. Grow en masse in humus-rich soil. Plants tend to perform well for a year or two, then get leggy and need replacing. Pull them out of the ground roots and all, take cuttings, refresh the soil, and replant.

Cotyledon

Plants in the genus *Cotyledon* are often confused with jade (*Crassula ovata*), but jades produce clusters of small star-shaped white or pink flowers in midwinter; cotyledons send up panicles of orange bell-shaped blooms in summer or fall. *Cotyledon orbiculata* attains 1 to 2 feet in height and has spatula-shaped or fingerlike leaves that, depending on the variety, may be gray or green, blushed

Cotyledon orbiculata var. oblonga 'Macrantha'

Crassula capitella 'Camp-fire' smolders between blue echeverias and peach-hued graptosedums.

Crassula sarcocaulis (bonsai crassula) underplanted with C. pubescens subsp. radicans in bloom

LEFT *Crassula corymbulosa* 'Red Pagoda' flows over the rim of a pot that also contains *C. perforata* 'Variegata', sunset jade, and *Sedum* ×*rubrotinctum* (both 'Aurora' and 'Pork and Beans').

ABOVE *Crassula multicava* in bloom

or edged with red, and/or farinose (covered with white powder). Hardy to the mid-20s F.

Cotyledon tomentosa (bear paws, kitten paws) forms a minishrub consisting of stems 12 to 18 inches long. Plump, fuzzy leaves tipped with reddish brown points suggest claws but are soft. Best grown in containers. A variegated form has cream-colored streaks.

Crassula

Crassula is a large and diverse genus of succulents with widely differing forms. Some, like jade (*C. ovata*), are trunk forming and shrublike. Others have stacked leaves threaded along ever-lengthening stems. These two types may seem like they don't belong in the same genus, but the key determinant is the flowers, which are tiny, star-shaped, and clustering.

Most crassulas will show frost damage on leaf tips at 32°F; if temperatures drop lower, unprotected foliage and stems will freeze, turn putty colored, and wither. Cut off the damaged parts, and the plants will recover. *Crassula sarcocaulis* (bonsai crassula) is unusual in that it's hardy to 15°F.

Crassula capitella 'Campfire', sometimes confused with similar (but smaller and more symmetrical) *C. corymbulosa* 'Red Pagoda', has pointed yellow-green leaves that turn bright red in full sun. Cut plants back to maintain compactness and encourage branching.

Crassula multicava (to 2 feet) is a no-fuss trailing ground cover that thrives in shady areas. Dark green oval leaves appear in pairs along ever-lengthening, floppy stems. In spring, white star-shaped flowers appear. If not frost burned or deadheaded, these produce plantlets that root when they touch the ground, enabling the plant to spread. *Crassula multicava* is seldom sold in nurseries because it's common and cuttings are easy to come by. Some gardeners find it a nuisance, but others welcome its lush and rapid growth.

Crassula ovata (also sold as *C. argentea*), commonly called jade plant, is perhaps the best-known shrub succulent and is grown worldwide as a houseplant. In frost-free climates, it's sometimes the only survivor in a neglected garden and thrives in vacant lots and alongside roadways. Should you be blessed with an old jade, prune it to show its branching structure, then use it as a backdrop plant or focal point of a garden bed. Glossy, oval green leaves redden when the plant is given full sun and minimal water.

Crassula ovata 'Gollum' at top, 'Tricolor' at right, and 'Hummel's Sunset' below

Crassula ovata 'Hobbit'

Crassula perfoliata var. *falcata*

Rather than trim and replant an old grouping of *Crassula tetragona* in my garden, I set a bottle fish in its midst.

In my three-tiered "stacked crassulas in stacked pots" composition, *Crassula perforata*, in bloom, is accompanied by smaller, greener *C. perforata* 'Variegata' and red-edged *C. rupestris*. Flapjack plants (*Kalanchoe luciae*) also look stacked and repeat the orange-red of the pots.

Dasylirion wheeleri in Jeff Pavlat's Texas garden shares a terrace with comparably winter-hardy *Agave ovatifolia* (far left), *A. ocahui* (center), and *A. xylonacantha* (right).

Dasylirion acrotrichum with golden barrel cacti (*Echinocactus grusonii*)

Jade starts easily from cuttings, grows over time to 4 or 5 feet in diameter and 3 or 4 feet tall, and produces clusters of star-shaped pink or pinkish white flowers in midwinter. The cultivar 'Hummel's Sunset' (sunset jade) blends yellow, orange, and touches of green in its foliage. The more sun, the more colorful it gets; in shade, it reverts to green. 'Tricolor' has white-and-green stripes (blushed with pink if sun is adequate). *Crassula ovata* 'Gollum' and 'Hobbit' have spoon-shaped depressions on leaf tips. ('Gollum' is more cylindrical, while 'Hobbit' leaves resemble sows' ears.)

Crassula perfoliata var. *falcata* (also sold as *C. falcata*), to 2 feet high and 2½ feet wide, is commonly called propeller plant because of its bladelike leaves. Greenish gray foliage contrasts with cinnamon-scented crimson flower clusters that appear in summer. Varieties with green or chartreuse leaves and orange flowers also exist.

Most common of the stacked crassulas are *Crassula perforata* and *C. rupestris*, two similar species with triangular leaves that overlap at right angles to each other, giving the look of stacked squares. Blooms grow from tips of stems that can attain 18 inches in length.

Crassula tetragona resembles a miniature pine tree, its trunk packed with regularly spaced, slender, inch-long pointed leaves. Eventually the plant will grow to several feet tall and branch. Creamy yellow flower clusters appear in late spring. If you don't like the look of denuded stems that get awkwardly long over time, take cuttings from the top, discard the plants (roots and all), and start afresh.

Dasylirion

Dasylirions lend great texture to any landscape. The plants, which grow into 5-foot-wide pincushions and are trunk forming over time, have long, stiff, ribbonlike leaves that shimmer in the breeze. The succulent aspect of dasylirions is their pineapple-like, water-storing cores. Native to southern Arizona, New Mexico, and northern Mexico, dasylirions handle frost, harsh sun, and temperatures down to the midteens F. Sometimes called sotols, dasylirions prefer full sun but will tolerate partial shade (though likely will not bloom).

Give dasylirions plenty of space so they won't need trimming, which would spoil their symmetry. Remove fallen leaves from plants' centers with a slender stick. Snip the plant's own dry leaves flush to its trunk.

Frayed tips of *Dasylirion acrotrichum* form delicate, translucent white curls. *Dasylirion longissimum* has dark green, whiplike foliage; *D. wheeleri*, inch-wide silvery gray

Dasylirion longissimum in bloom

Blue *Senecio mandraliscae* and red-flowered *Euphorbia milii* complement a specimen of *Dracaena draco* in this La Jolla, California, front yard.

leaves with toothed margins. When mature, dasylirions bloom in summer, producing one or more flower stalks that grow upwards of 5 feet tall. Tiny flowers held densely against the top of the stalk give them a cotton-swab silhouette.

Dracaena

Native to the Canary Islands off the coast of Morocco, *Dracaena draco* grows well in mild-climate coastal gardens. A thick, cylindrical trunk with horizontal bands branches into stout arms, each ending in clusters of stiff, lancelike leaves. The red in the bands is a reminder that the trees bleed crimson sap when cut—perhaps the reason for the common name, dragon tree.

Succulent trees such as *Dracaena draco* tend to be slow growing compared to woody trees, so large specimens are uncommon and expensive. The largest on record is 70 feet tall, but 30 feet (with a crown nearly as wide) is more likely in cultivation. Sprays of cream-colored flowers that rise above the trees in summer are followed by marble-size fruits. Hardy to the low 30s F; susceptible to root rot if watered in summer.

Dudleya

There's nothing quite like a foot-wide, silvery white dudleya rosette with long bloom stalks radiating from its base. Chalky rosettes of some dudleyas resemble those of echeverias, and even their flowers look similar, but although the two groups are in the same family, they are not close enough to hybridize. Notice how dudleyas grow in their habitat (west of the Rockies): on cliff sides and escarpments. They're native to marine-influenced areas of Oregon and California, as well as to Arizona, Nevada, and Baja California. Give these winter growers superb drainage and no summer irrigation. Expect dudleyas to look dry and sad in summer, and resist the temptation to rescue a rosette by watering it or peeling away its dry leaves. These persist on the stem to protect it from summer heat, sun, and desiccation. However, they also can harbor mealybugs introduced by Argentine ants in late summer, so watch for signs of infestation and spray leaf axils with isopropyl alcohol if need be.

Of dozens of *Dudleya* species, few are in cultivation, and many are rare. *Dudleya brittonii* (to 12 inches high and wide), native to coastal southern California and northern Mexico, and *D. hassei*, native to Catalina Island, are perhaps the best known and most often seen in gardens. Dudleyas are variable and can be difficult to identify, even by experts.

Dudleya hassei (front left) with two specimens of *D. brittonii.*

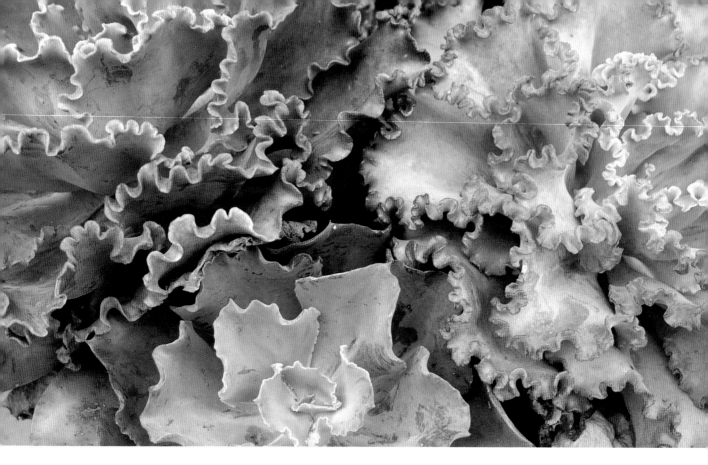

Echeveria cultivars with ruffled edges come in hues ranging from soft pastels to jewel tones, and some may even combine the colors.

Echeveria

Of all succulents, echeverias tend to be the ones that seduce flower lovers first. The plants look like fleshy roses yet come in colors roses don't, such as light blue and green, as well as pastel and deep shades of pink, lavender, teal, brown, red, orange, dove gray, and tan—occasionally in combination. Leaf textures include smooth, powdery, bumpy, and furry. Shape and thickness of leaves vary from thin discs to pointed wedges, nearly always in a whorl.

Flower stalks of echeverias are tall relative to the plants, shaped like question marks, and lined with bell-shaped blooms in shades of yellow, coral, pink, orange, or rose red. The genus includes more than 150 species, which range in size from ping-pong balls to basketballs. Some are solitary, others colony forming. Native to the Americas, mainly Mexico, they were named after eighteenth-century botanical artist Atanasio Echeverría y Godoy.

In their native habitats, echeverias grow on rocky outcroppings where water drains rapidly away from the roots. This means they're never waterlogged—an important clue to keeping them healthy in captivity. Echeverias don't require full sun but should be given enough bright light to prevent etiolation (stretching), which spoils what we love about them: their symmetry. Several hours of morning or afternoon sun (with dappled shade in the heat of the day) make echeverias more beautiful by bringing out red or pink tones in their leaves. Too much sun can cause beige or brown patches.

I've found the plants tend to do best in containers, where they can be monitored and repositioned as needed. A time-lapse video of my deck

Echeveria 'Afterglow'

Echeveria agavoides 'Lipstick'

Echeveria setosa (the species name means bristly)

Echeveria imbricata

Pots of *Echeveria* 'Cubic Frost' sit atop a low stone wall in my garden. Nearby are burgundy *Aeonium* 'Jack Catlin', blue *Lampranthus deltoides*, and yellow-orange *Sedum nussbaumerianum*.

Euphorbia polygona 'Snowflake'

throughout the year would show echeverias zipping all over the place: in a corner for sun protection, closer to the railing for greater sun, rotated to keep bud spikes perpendicular, beneath a bench for frost protection, out in the open during a rainstorm, arranged atop a table when guests are coming, then quarantined in another corner after being treated for mealybugs.

Most echeverias prefer mild temperatures, but a few are surprisingly hardy, at least for short periods. Among those unfazed by frosty nights in the mid-20s F (if dry) are *Echeveria* 'Afterglow', which has pale lavender leaves thinly margined in red; *E. agavoides*, so named because its thick, triangular leaves are pointed like those of agaves; widely grown, pale blue *E. elegans*; sky-blue *E. imbricata*, which produces hen-and-chicks offsets; and perfectly pink *E.* 'Perle von Nürnberg'.

The showiest of echeveria cultivars resemble cabbage roses and indeed are as large as cabbages. Some have ruffled edges; a few are weirdly bumpy (caruncled). Major growers introduce new cultivars every year. One favorite is *Echeveria* 'Cubic Frost', a lavender version of dove-gray 'Topsy Turvy' created by hybridizer Renee O'Connell and patented by Altman Plants. It makes guests gasp.

Euphorbia

Euphorbia is a huge genus composed of plants with milky sap, including spurges and poinsettias. Those that are succulents range from marble-size spheres to 30-foot trees. Their sap can be mildly to severely irritating to the skin, depending on the variety. (Don't grow euphorbias in areas where children play.) Euphorbias are good examples of this rule of thumb: the more moisture a plant stores, the less tolerant it is of overwatering and the longer it can go without water. Some species store moisture as efficiently as cacti. The majority of euphorbias that form stems or trunks are frost tender.

Although many succulent euphorbias resemble cacti because of their columnar or spherical forms, lack of leaves, and thorns, cacti come from the Americas and succulent euphorbias from the Old World (mainly Africa). While flowers of cacti are large in proportion to the plant and usually vividly colored, flowers of euphorbias are tiny relative to the plant and most often yellow, though some are white, purple, or rusty red. Euphorbia flowers are followed by beadlike seed capsules. Spines of cacti radiate from growth points called areoles; thorns

BELOW *Euphorbia obesa* may look like a cactus, but its itty-bitty blooms give it away.

RIGHT *Euphorbia ammak* 'Variegata' with golden barrel cacti

on euphorbias (which are not vestigial leaves) emerge directly from the body of the plant, often in pairs. A few succulent euphorbias (including *Euphorbia ingens*, *E. milii*, and *E. trigona*) have both leaves and thorns.

Among those euphorbias useful for adding height and vertical interest to mild-climate landscapes are tall, statuesque varieties that resemble columnar cacti and impart to gardens a Southwest ambience. Numerous types are available—some smooth, others spiky—but those found in nurseries are primarily *Euphorbia ammak* and *E. ingens*. These start out single trunked and as they age become massively branched, to 20 feet or more in height and spread.

Medusoid euphorbias are so named because numerous cylindrical arms that emerge from their central heads are reminiscent of the mythological Medusa, who had snakes for hair. These bumpy green stems radiate from the core of the plant in a Fibonacci spiral. Tiny yellow, white, or red flowers appear at the tips of the arms.

Fat, cylindrical *Euphorbia polygona* 'Snowflake' has vertical ridges and furrows that in some specimens are wavy, as though collapsing beneath their own weight. The cultivar name comes from the plants' silvery skin and star-shaped tops. Grows slowly over time to about 2 feet tall and produces offsets; hardy to 25°F.

Euphorbia milii (to 4 feet tall and 2 feet wide) blooms almost nonstop. Commonly called crown of thorns, the woody shrubs have stems that are spiky like those of rose bushes. The plants provide textural contrast to smooth and soft-leaved succulents but are most valued for colorful bracts that resemble flower petals. These cup the actual flowers, which are tiny and form on branch tips. From a distance, the plants' red, pink, yellow, white, or coral bracts framed by green or reddish leaves suggest geraniums. Numerous hybrids exhibit variations of size, growth habit, and color.

Euphorbia resinifera (to 18 inches high), from Morocco, forms tight clumps of inch-thick, four-sided, upright cylinders. Hardy to 20°F (for short periods). As the species name suggests, it does indeed have resinous sap.

Few plants offer the bright punch of orange, pink, and red provided by *Euphorbia tirucalli* 'Sticks on Fire' (to 5 feet tall and wide). This South African native resembles a leafless shrub with multiple upright, cylindrical branches. Its color is not due to environmental stress but rather a beneficial virus. To keep it bright, give it full sun and fertilize in spring and fall.

Wherever you plant 'Sticks on Fire', it calls attention to itself. Use it to lend height to garden beds and containers. To suggest a bonfire, plant it in a saucer-shaped concrete pot—or perhaps in an unused fire pit—with crushed lava rock at its base. Combine it with aloes and

perennials with the same blend of sunset hues (such as *Gazania* hybrids) or contrast it with cobalt-blue lobelia, purple *Tradescantia pallida* 'Purpurea', or any succulent with blue-green leaves.

Euphorbia trigona, native to tropical western Africa, is often used as a potted plant, indoors and out. 'Rubra' has stems marbled with white and green, with red tips. Attains 6 feet over time.

Closely related to *Euphorbia* are succulents in the genus *Pedilanthus*, commonly called lady's slipper because of the shape of the blooms. *Pedilanthus* species, which have cylindrical green or gray-green stems, are useful for adding upright interest to pots and garden beds. Like euphorbias, they also have milky, toxic sap. Hardiness varies according to species.

Euphorbia ingens

Euphorbia gorgonis, one of the medusoid euphorbias

Euphorbia resinifera

Euphorbia tirucalli 'Sticks on Fire' combines with *Aeonium* 'Sunburst' and with 'Sunset' and 'Tricolor' jades in Lila Yee's mild-climate garden. Red dots at far left middle are bracts of a dwarf *Euphorbia milii* cultivar.

Euphorbia trigona is framed by a red-leaved, nonsucculent tree in the same genus, *E. cotinifolia*.

Furcraea foetida 'Mediopicta', with *Agave weberi* at left and
A. angustifolia 'Marginata' at right

Furcraea

Furcraeas, like agaves (they're in the same family), form
large, fountain-shaped rosettes and are monocarpic (they
die after flowering). *Furcraea foetida* 'Mediopicta' (to 5 feet)
has cream to yellow stripes on leaves with green margins.
Its long, tapered leaves are more pliable than those of most
agaves (*Agave attenuata* being one exception) and not as
thick. Furcraeas are susceptible to sunburn and frost damage, and do best in mild maritime climates such as coastal
California, Florida, and Hawaii.

Gasteria acinicifolia (12 inches in diameter) in bloom

Gasteria

Gasterias are useful in pots and rock gardens, and can be grown indoors. They
prefer dappled shade and, similar to the haworthias to which they're related,
are susceptible to sunburn. Hardiness depends on species, but most gasterias do fine into the mid-20s F. The name comes from the shape of the flowers,
which resemble little stomachs; these dangle along slender, arching stems in

×*Gasteraloe* 'Green Ice'

×*Graptoveria* 'Fred Ives' with *Lampranthus deltoides*

spring and summer. It's unusual to see a gasteria in cultivation bigger than 6 inches high and 12 inches wide, although some do get much larger under ideal conditions. These collectible succulents have thick, stiff leaves that form stemless rosettes. Colors range from green through shades of gray, and some are speckled with white dots or reddish blotches and may be textured kind of like sandpaper. Take care not to break leaves or let snails get to them; the beauty of gasterias is in their symmetry, and they keep what few leaves they have for years.

×*Gasteraloe* 'Green Ice', an intergeneric cross between *Gasteria* and *Aloe*, is more tolerant of overwatering than the typical gasteria, and a good plant for beginners. Each specimen's light-and-dark-green variegations are slightly different. Protect from Argentine ants in autumn.

Graptopetalum

Graptopetalum rosettes resemble echeverias, to which they are related. *Graptopetalum paraguayense* (from Mexico, not Paraguay) has silvery gray rosettes of oval leaves that are pointed at the tips and covered with a powdery film. Plants turn gray-blue when grown in shade and take on tinges of lavender, pink, and yellow in more sun. Leaves break off easily and will root and form new little plants. Use as a trailing succulent in tall pots and terraces or as a ground cover for areas that receive no foot traffic. Intergeneric hybrids produced by crossing *Graptopetalum* and *Echeveria* are known as ×*Graptoveria*.

A pot for a low-light area features hawor-thias (notably white-banded *Haworthia attenuata* and, at far right, bright green *H. retusa*), along with *Gasteria bicolor* var. *liliputana* (foreground left).

Haworthia

Haworthias are low-light succulents well suited to containers. The various types might be loosely classified as those with thin, pointed leaves and those with thick, sometimes windowed leaves that resemble molded gelatin. Those that offset, which is the majority, form tight colonies that grow so closely together that rosettes overlap. Haworthias seldom get much larger than softballs. Native to South Africa, they tend to slow down or stop growing in the hottest part of the summer and the coldest part of the winter. Widely grown *Haworthia attenuata* suggests a miniature agave banded with raised white ridges; its common name is zebra plant. Perhaps the most popular of the windowed varieties is *H. retusa*, which forms a tight rosette of wedge-shaped green leaves.

Haworthias and gasterias are closely related and share similar cultivation requirements, and collectors of one genus often collect the other. Because of their small size and preference for bright shade, both make wonderful windowsill plants. Rotate the pots 180 degrees twice monthly for even light exposure. Water once a week during active growth and not at all during summer dormancy. If you don't like the look of the plants' skinny, whiplike bloom stalks, snip them off—I do.

Hesperaloe parviflora with dusty miller

Hesperaloe

Hesperaloes, long popular in Arizona and New Mexico landscapes, are showing up more in dry California gardens. Plants that attain 3 or 4 feet in height produce airy spires of pink or yellow tubular blooms several feet tall in summer. Leaves are upright and strappy, with white filaments that peel away from the edges. The succulent aspect of hesperaloes is their water-storing core. The similarity of the buds to those of aloes inspired the plant's name—*Hesperaloe* means aloe of the West. Offsets grow around the mother plant in a hen-and-chicks fashion.

The common name of red yucca is applied to the popular species *Hesperaloe parviflora* because of its reddish flowers and leaves with curling threads that call to mind its relatives the yuccas. Varieties that produce cream or yellow blooms are also available. Plants are cold hardy to 0°F, possibly lower. Give full sun and supplemental irrigation in summer to encourage flowering. Good for desert gardens.

In a streetside garden, orange and yellow *Lampranthus aurantiacus*, magenta *L. spectabilis*, and pink *Drosanthemum floribundum* sing together in spring. Companion plants include euryops daisies and purple statice (*Limonium perezii*).

Fenestraria rhopalophylla subsp. *aurantiaca* (baby toes, window plant, also sold as *Fenestraria aurantiaca*)

Ice Plants

The name *ice plant* likely comes from the appearance of the leaves of certain varieties, which appear coated with ice crystals. These succulents produce neon-bright flowers for several weeks in spring. The rest of the year they form a green or gray-blue mass with a smattering of blooms. Do mix flower colors; such combinations are simple, low maintenance, and eye popping.

Ground covers formerly classified as *Mesembryanthemum* (and commonly called mesembs or ice plants) include *Delosperma*, *Drosanthemum*, *Malephora*, and *Lampranthus*. Stems can reach several feet in length and form shrubby mounds. Ice plants cannot be walked on, but they make great ground covers for slopes and other low-traffic areas. They fill in so densely they discourage weed growth and help prevent erosion.

Ice plants are hardy to the mid-20s F, and some go much lower. Delospermas, for example, are hardy to −10°F. Most ice plants are fine in temperatures into the 90s F if given regular water, but they seldom thrive in desert regions. *Drosanthemum floribundum* (rosea or floribunda ice plant) is common in California; its overlapping dime-size blooms are shades of magenta or lavender-pink.

When mimicry plants (living stones, split rocks, window plants, and more) bloom, their shimmering, daisylike flowers reveal that they too are ice plants. In their arid African habitats, certain varieties, such as *Lithops* and *Fenestraria* species, are nearly buried; sunlight reaches photosynthetic cells inside the plants via their windowed tips. Others, such as *Pleiospilos* and *Dinteranthus* species, blend in with their pebbled habitats. Mimicry plants need excellent drainage and appreciate a mix of two-thirds pumice and one-third potting soil. It's a rite of passage for novice enthusiasts to fail to cultivate them successfully. The key, in addition to the right soil, is to know a given species' growing and resting periods and to water accordingly.

Alongside a red-flowering *Kalanchoe blossfeldiana* cultivar is gray-leaved, pink-flowering *K. pumila*.

Kalanchoe beharensis and variegated sansevierias

Kalanchoe

Leaves of *Kalanchoe* species have intriguing shapes and textures—from smooth, green, and glossy to nubby, silvery gray, and scalloped. Flowers vary from clusters of tiny stars to bean-size bells on multibranched stalks. The plants develop roots and leaves in spring and summer, and then flower in autumn and winter. The majority are from Madagascar. Give them water during warm weather when the soil is dry and then withhold it during the winter when temperatures drop below 50°F.

Kalanchoes in the subcategory bryophyllum are characterized by leaf margins lined with tiny plantlets. When they fall off, given the right conditions (which is pretty much anything), they take root. So, is this a good thing? Perhaps not. Maybe they're weeds—until they mature and produce glorious umbels of pendant, tubular orange flowers.

Kalanchoes seldom get larger than 2 feet tall, with the notable exception of *Kalanchoe beharensis* (felt bush, to 6 feet; rarely, 9 feet or more). Display it as a specimen tree, either in a protected area of the garden or in a large pot. Its stiff, arrowhead-shaped leaves grow several feet long and appear made of gray-green felt. In late winter, the plant produces panicles of small yellow-green flowers.

Look for *Kalanchoe blossfeldiana* (supermarket kalanchoe, to 12 inches high and wide) in garden centers and supermarkets in spring and autumn.

Kalanchoe tubiflora (also sold as *K. delagoensis*, *Bryophyllum delagoense*)

When *Kalanchoe luciae* is grown in full sun, its oval leaves turn bright red. In less light, they become larger and revert to green.

Kalanchoe orgyalis

Kalanchoe tomentosa

Kalanchoe fedtschenkoi 'Variegata' thrives
in Claire Chao's garden in Honolulu, Hawaii.

OPPOSITE *Kalanchoe* 'Pink Butterflies'

The species, which has been extensively hybridized, is arguably the most commercial succulent and the only one sold for its flowers. The compact plants have shiny, scalloped dark green leaves and masses of hot-hued blooms. Although sold as a houseplant, *K. blossfeldiana* can also be grown outside in mild-climate gardens where frost and scorching sun are not concerns. Pinch off old flowers to encourage an encore. Plants do tend to bloom themselves to death, so if a favorite starts going downhill, take cuttings and start it afresh.

With its lavender-pink foliage and peach-colored, pendant flowers, *Kalanchoe fedtschenkoi* is worth having and easy to grow in mild climates. Best when massed. Attains 18 inches in height when in bloom.

Its foliage alone makes growing *Kalanchoe luciae* worthwhile. Commonly called paddle plant or flapjack plant, the South African native's blue-green oval leaves are edged in red. (The more sun, the redder the leaves.) The center elongates when it blooms, creating a silhouette reminiscent of a

A pink cultivar of *Lewisia cotyledon*.

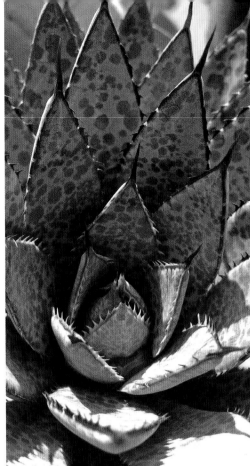

×*Mangave* 'Blood Spot'

minaret. Since flowers sap the plant's energy, some gardeners remove the flowering stalks as they emerge; this maintains the plant's compact shape and encourages new growth. (Pinch out new bloom spikes that will continue to form in leaf axils for several weeks.) *Kalanchoe luciae* is often mislabeled *K. thyrsiflora*, which is similar but lacks the pronounced red color that makes *K. luciae* so striking.

Kalanchoe orgyalis (to 3 feet) has spoon-shaped, velvety bicolored leaves. These emerge rust brown and, as they age, turn silvery green with pale gray undersides.

Kalanchoe 'Pink Butterflies' is ruffled with pink plantlets in summer. These won't thrive because they lack chlorophyll, but they do make an intriguing plant that in itself resembles a flower. I've yet to see 'Pink Butterflies' bloom, but flowers aren't the point, are they?

Kalanchoe tomentosa (panda plant, to 18 inches high) has fuzzy leaves that suggest the ears of a plush rabbit, with brown stitching along the edges. Flowers are small, furry yellow-brown bells. Due to its size, texture, and silvery color, this makes a wonderful container plant, either in combination with other succulents or solo. Cultivars come in shades of gold and brown.

Lewisia

Lewisia, named after its discoverer, explorer Meriwether Lewis, is an alpine wildflower native to western North America. The perennials, which have dark green leaves, produce satiny white, pink, or apricot-hued flowers atop 12-inch burgundy-red stems in spring and summer (year-round along the coast). *Lewisia cotyledon*, readily available in Pacific Northwest nurseries, serves as a showy rock garden plant, especially when those of different flower colors are combined. Provide excellent drainage and semishade or dappled sun. Water minimally in winter or plants may rot. Hardy to zone 3; difficult to grow in the Southwest.

Mangave

If plants can be fashionable, the latest stars are mangaves, intergeneric hybrids of *Manfreda* and *Agave*. Introduced during the first decade of the twenty-first century, mangaves are noteworthy for their unusual

×*Mangave* 'Macho Mocha' coming into bloom

Orostachys malacophylla var. *iwarenge*

Othonna capensis

coloration. ×*Mangave* 'Blood Spot' (to 12 inches in diameter, hardy to 10°F) is a symmetrical rosette of stiff, narrow, red-toothed gray leaves blotched with red. Those of larger 'Macho Mocha' are more flexible, curve up and out, and are purple-green.

Orostachys

The twelve or so accepted species in the genus *Orostachys* are diminutive succulents suited to cold-climate rock gardens, miniature gardens, and containers. Gray or green rosettes spread to form a dense mat. In autumn, rosettes elongate into conical flower spikes that suggest wizards' hats. Rosettes are monocarpic (die after flowering), but offsets take their place. These biennials are native to northern China, Japan, Korea, Mongolia, and Russia. All are hardy to below zero, some as low as −32°F. Plants grow best in well-drained soil and partial shade. The common name is Chinese dunce cap, but I refuse to call them that.

Othonna

Othonna capensis, from South Africa, looks like a cross between an ice plant and a ground-cover senecio. Its inch-long, juicy green leaves blush to shades of rose and lavender when environmentally stressed. Flowers resemble those of senecios in that they're dime-size and yellow, and become white fluff when finished. However, othonna flowers are not as messy, are held closer to the plant, are more prolific, and bloom on and off year-round.

Stems of *Othonna capensis* are thinner than those of senecios and not as tough as those of ice plants. As old leaves wither and fall off ever-lengthening stems, they become denuded and bake in the sun, which compromises their ability to transmit water and nutrients. Trim the damaged stems, keep healthy tips, and replant as cuttings.

Othonna capensis grows rapidly; a 4-inch potful becomes a 12-inch-diameter clump in a year. It does well in the ground for several years before needing rejuvenation and makes an excellent filler for container gardens.

Pachypodium lamerei

Portulacaria afra 'Variegata' is interplanted with blue *Senecio mandraliscae* at Huntington Botanical Gardens.

Pachypodium

Pachypodium lamerei has a spiny, bulbous trunk topped by lancelike foot-long leaves. Although commonly called Madagascar palm, it's not related to true palms. *Pachypodium lamerei* may reach a height of 18 feet or more in subtropical climates but will do well indoors in bright light in colder areas. In the garden it can take a mild frost, though growth may be stunted, and it prefers regular water except during winter dormancy. When mature, trees produce fragrant flowers that resemble those of their relatives the plumerias, followed by seedpods that look like brown bananas.

Portulacaria

Portulacaria afra, commonly called elephant's food, provides as much as 80 percent of the diet of elephants. The large animals inadvertently propagate it by breaking its branches, which root readily and form new stands. The species is often confused with jade (*Crassula ovata*) because both have oval green leaves, but portulacaria leaves are smaller (dime size), and new stems are red and don't snap off as easily. *Portulacaria afra* also has a looser shape consisting of numerous stems that grow in random directions, giving plants a bad-hair-day look.

Portulacaria afra grows 6 to 8 feet tall and wide, and makes a good hedge or screen. Yellow-and-green *Portulacaria afra* 'Variegata' stays low and spreading and is an excellent, fuss-free ornamental shrub and pot filler. Two diminutive prostrate forms, one with green foliage and the other with new leaves that are yellow, serve well as mounding ground covers and cascaders. Unless kept very dry, *Portulacaria afra* won't produce sprays of delicate lavender-pink flowers. It does well in desert gardens if protected from hot afternoon sun and is a good plant for bonsai because of its wiry, flexible stems. An uncommon larger variety has thicker stems and bigger green leaves.

Portulacaria afra

Sansevieria trifasciata underplanted with tropical cacti and violas.

In a Bellingham, Washington, garden, *Sedum* 'Autumn Joy' (now named 'Herbstfreude') provides color, texture, and a long bloom show. With this shrub sedum are purple asters, white alyssum, and lavender-hued *Salvia officinalis*.

Sansevieria

The more than 130 species and cultivars of *Sansevieria*, commonly called mother-in-law's tongue or snake plant, have upright, stiff, pointed leaves. These can be shaped like triangles, straps, or cylinders; can be thin, wide, or guttered; come in every shade of green; and may be striped or banded with shades of yellow, gray, and/or cream. Tall varieties are effective when grown in multiples; position them along the base of a wall and use as vertical accents for container gardens.

Sansevierias are remarkably tolerant of neglect and thrive indoors, in pots, with minimal light and water. Certain species, such as *Sansevieria trifasciata*, of which there are sixty cultivars ranging from 2 to 4 feet tall, do fine in full morning sun in mild maritime climates; others may sunburn unless in full to partial shade. Protect from frost and give well-drained, sandy soil. Water regularly during warm months and not at all during cool. Don't place a sansevieria where a pet might chew the leaves, as they contain saponins that are toxic to dogs and cats.

Sedum

The numerous species of the genus *Sedum* can be loosely divided into three types. Cold-hardy, tiny-leaved stonecrops need protection from sun in the Southwest but can handle temperatures down to the single digits (or lower) in northern climates. Showy, all-climate shrub sedums bloom in autumn and die to the ground in winter. And Mexican sedums with thumbnail-size or larger leaves handle heat but may be damaged at temperatures below 30°F. Flower clusters of all sedums—large or small—can be so abundant they hide the foliage.

Sedums with rice-size leaves or dainty rosettes are found in rocky terrains, hence the common name stonecrop. They do well tucked into the niches of stone walls, where their roots anchor them, they're never waterlogged, and their stems can cascade. Small stonecrops make good fillers for container compositions, topiaries, vertical gardens, patterned plantings, and wreaths. They're also a key component of green roofs in northern climates. Small stonecrops are heat sensitive, so

Sedums and graptosedums surround pink-tipped blue echeverias in poolside pots. Sun brings out jewel tones in the plants' leaves.

Sedum rupestre 'Angelina' (Angelina stone-crop) adds feathery texture to a fountain that also contains burro tail (*S. burrito*) and red-blushed *S.* ×*rubrotinctum* 'Pork and Beans'.

An alpine trough garden includes two new sedums in hybridizer-designer Chris Hansen's registered SunSparkler line: 'Lime Twister' (variegated plant in the center) and 'Sedoro Blue Elf' (at left). Accompanying them are *Sedum album* 'Coral Carpet' (lower right corner) and *S. rupestre* 'Angelina' (upper right), red-and-green *Sempervivum hookeri* (foreground center), dark green *Sempervivum* 'Oddity' (behind 'Lime Twister'), and *Sempervivum allionii* (upper left corner).

Sedum burrito (burro tail), left; *S. morganianum* (donkey tail), right

in regions with summers that rise into the 80s F and higher, don't deadhead the plants after they bloom; the spent flowers will help shade the plants. Cut back when the weather cools.

Sedum morganianum (donkey tail) has ever-lengthening stems covered with overlapping bullet-shaped leaves that pop off easily. From a distance, stems appear braided. It seems interchangeable with *S. burrito* (burro tail) until you see the two together; the latter has shorter, fatter leaves that cling better. Donkey tail is seldom sold in nurseries due to its fragility, but it's common in gardens because of the ease with which fallen leaves form new plants.

Few succulents offer the bold orange-gold of *Sedum nussbaumerianum* (rosettes to 3 inches in diameter). Although it forms lovely clumps, it eventually gets leggy. Growth is on stem tips, and as older leaves shrivel, stems become denuded. Uproot and discard old plants and restart the rosettes as cuttings.

Among the most versatile sedums is Angelina stonecrop (*Sedum rupestre* 'Angelina'), which will grow nearly anywhere. It's hardy to 0°F yet handles temperatures into the 90s F (if shaded). Its color changes from chartreuse to gold depending on how much sun it gets. When environmentally stressed, leaf tips turn orange. Use 'Angelina' to create rivers of color in flower beds, as a ground cover between stepping-stones, and juxtaposed with plants with deep red flowers or foliage. It's also lovely cascading from containers and retaining walls.

Sedum spurium and its cultivars (zones 4 through 9) are ground huggers with inch-long green, bronzy, or variegated leaves. Plants spread to 2 feet or more. In late summer, bud clusters appear and mature into pink flowers. *Sedum spurium* 'Tricolor' is variegated green, cream, and rosy pink.

Shrub sedums grow to 18 inches or more in height. Rising atop slender stems in late summer are domed and showy flower heads that deepen in color as autumn

BELOW Orange-gold *Sedum nussbaumerianum* stands out against the backdrop of a dark green dwarf sedum. At lower right is bright yellow *S. makinoi* 'Ogon'.

RIGHT In a rock garden constructed of broken and stained chunks of concrete are *Sedum spurium* 'Tricolor' in bloom at top, *S. rupestre* 'Blue Spruce' at bottom (yellow flowers), and dainty *S. dasyphyllum* at middle left.

Hylotelephium 'Red Cauli' in New York City's High Line Park.

progresses. Let spent blooms dry on the plants; when winter comes, they're lovely covered in snow. Shrub sedums that thrive in zones 5 through 10 include *Hylotelephium* (formerly *Sedum telephium*) and its hybrids, which have foliage in various shades of green and blue-green, and flowers in sunset colors.

Graptosedums are intergeneric crosses of rosette succulents in the genera *Graptopetalum* and *Sedum*. When environmentally stressed, cultivars turn vibrant hues of chartreuse, gold, coral, bronze, mauve, burgundy, and rose. Although they get leggy over time, graptosedums do branch and propagate easily from cuttings and fallen leaves.

Sempervivum arachnoideum

OPPOSITE Vancouver, British Columbia, designer Todd Holloway combined red, blue, red-and-blue, and white-webbed sempervivums in a wide, shallow pot—repetition at its finest.

Sempervivum

If you live in a northerly climate that's too cold to grow most succulents outdoors year-round, you can likely grow sempervivums (commonly called hen-and-chicks, a name also used for echeverias). The genus *Sempervivum* includes around forty species and more than three thousand cultivars, with symmetrical rosettes that are a few inches across and spread to a foot or more. Native to the mountains of Europe, sempervivums prefer cool, dry locations. Most species will grow outdoors year-round in zones 4 through 7. Colors vary from shades of green and blue through deep burgundy, and many are bicolored.

Semps have thin, pointed leaves and produce ball-shaped babies that nestle around the mother plant, attached to it by slender stems. Once the little plants root, they become independent. When a rosette flowers, it dies, but plants grow so tightly together that the loss is seldom noticeable. Given ideal conditions, the ever-expanding colonies flow over terraces and hug the pockets of stone walls, rock gardens, and strawberry jars.

Sempervivum arachnoideum (commonly called cobweb houseleek), zones 5 through 10 (if shaded), has pointed leaf tips webbed with white threads. By collecting dew, the filaments help keep the plant hydrated.

Sempervivum includes what used to be a separate genus, *Jovibarba*. Plants look similar but jovibarbas have bell-shaped pale yellow flowers; those of semps are flattened starbursts. Cultivation requirements are the same, except jovibarbas are not as tolerant of prolonged wet conditions.

ABOVE *Senecio mandraliscae* serves as a colorful, easy-care border for garden paths.

RIGHT *Senecio anteuphorbium*

Senecio

The thousand or so species that belong to the genus *Senecio* have in common daisylike flowers arranged in small clusters atop skinny stems. The few senecios that are succulents are grown for the shape and color of their leaves, seldom for their blooms, which dry into untidy, dandelion-like tufts. (Some gardeners snip the bloom stalks when they begin to form.) In mild climates, the plants spread readily but not invasively.

Senecio anteuphorbium consists of cylindrical, 1-inch-diameter, upright stems sparsely covered with small oval leaves. It grows to several feet tall and is good in large pots or as a vertical accent in the garden. Use it to suggest reeds in a dry creek bed. Frost hardy to the mid-20s F (if kept dry) and notably drought tolerant.

Senecio mandraliscae, to 8 inches high, is a full-sun ground cover in all but desert climates. Few plants, succulent or otherwise, have such a true blue color. Fingerlike, tapered leaves grow at the tips of ever-lengthening stems. Best planted in the ground, en masse; this is not an interesting potted plant. As it emerges from summer dormancy, cut stems back to encourage branching and use tips to fill bare spots. Hardy to 15°F.

Senecio rowleyanus (string of pearls) forms long strands of pea-size green beads that make it suited to hanging baskets, tall pots, and terraces. Protect from intense sun lest the plant's threadlike stems become scorched. Best suited to mild climates; in hotter areas substitute *S. radicans* (string of bananas, fish hooks). Strands of both species hang 6 feet long or more over time.

Senecio vitalis (also sold as *Senecio cylindricus*) has several-inch-long, upright leaves on stems that grow to 2 feet tall and form mounding shrubs 3 feet wide. Leaves are slender, tapered, and bright green-blue. This is a good backdrop shrub, but stems do sprawl. Keep it compact and encourage branching by trimming the top 6 inches once or twice a year.

Senecio vitalis contrasts with a taupe wall and *Crassula capitella* 'Campfire'.

FAR LEFT Beneath an aeonium valance, *Senecio radicans* serves as a whimsical window curtain at the Succulent Café in Oceanside, California.

LEFT At the Succulent Café, a ceramic pitcher pours *Senecio rowleyanus* (string of pearls) into a basin containing *Sedum rupestre* 'Angelina' and blue pachyphytums.

Yucca aloifolia

Yucca

Wherever you live, there's a yucca for you. Native to the Americas, yuccas grow from Central America to Canada and have naturalized worldwide. Species range from stemless rosettes to 40-foot trees. Some are hardy well below 0°F, and most are truly tough and hard to kill. In fact, that's the best and worst thing about them. Yuccas can be a little too easy to grow and once established may take over. But placed correctly, yuccas serve as ornamental trees that need almost no water or maintenance. Large bloom stalks are massed with waxy flowers that resemble whipped cream. The flowers are edible, but the root—though often said to be—is not. Yuca root (one *c*), from which tapioca is made, is very different. The succulent aspect of yuccas is their water-storing trunk or bulbous base.

Whenever I need an instant tree, I saw off a *Yucca aloifolia* (Spanish bayonet) limb. The wood is corky, so this can be done with a steak knife, and the limbs are so lightweight I can carry one that's 4 feet long in one hand. The deeper the stem is planted, the better, because roots emerge from where the trunk touches the soil. Even a cutting lying atop the ground will root, and from the horizontal trunk, new growth will turn upward. This species is among those that over time grow a massive base that can crack a home's foundation, retaining wall, or swimming pool, and break irrigation pipes. Position them carefully; once established, such plants are difficult to remove.

Compared to other succulent trees, yuccas are more common, faster growing, and less expensive. In a succulent landscape, the slender leaves of yuccas are useful for repeating the similar silhouettes of agaves, furcraeas, dasylirions, and aloes. Variegated yuccas are especially beautiful backlit by early morning or late afternoon sun.

Get new plants off to a good start with occasional deep soakings. Yuccas look more tidy if their dry, downward-pointing lower leaves are trimmed, but considering how knifelike these can be, it's a challenge—especially when leaf clusters are high off the ground. Yuccas don't drop a lot of leaf litter, but they don't provide much of a shade canopy either. Like all pointy succulents, yuccas should be positioned well away from walkways and children's play areas.

Perhaps the most ornamental species is *Yucca rostrata*, which over time forms a trunk topped by one or more shimmering pincushions of blue-gray leaves. Its lack of availability in nurseries is due to its glacially slow growth. Also on my wish list is *Y. aloifolia* 'Tricolor', which is cream-and-green striped, flushed with red. Like *Y. aloifolia*, it grows to 10 feet tall and 8 to 10 feet wide, is hardy to 15°F (or lower), needs no water once established, and is fine in full sun.

Yucca rostrata at the Denver Botanic Gardens

Yucca aloifolia 'Tricolor'

A Designer's Palette

Plant Lists for Succulent Gardens

If you're overwhelmed by the selection of succulents available or simply want to know your options in terms of size, color, and texture, these plant selections by category are a good place to start.

Tall, Treelike, and Immense Succulents

Large succulents provide beneficial microclimates for smaller plants and, compared to woody trees, create very little leaf litter. A solo dasylirion, with its fountainlike spray of slender leaves, or an agave the size of a Volkswagen are garden standouts, useful as backdrop plants and focal points. If you like a minimalist look, top-dress the ground with gravel and you're done.

Agave americana
Agave franzosinii
Agave ovatifolia
Agave salmiana
Agave weberi
Aloe barberae
Aloe ferox
Aloe 'Hercules'
Aloe marlothii
Aloe speciosa
beaucarneas

cacti, ceroid (columnar)
dasylirions
Dracaena draco
Euphorbia ammak
Euphorbia ingens
Euphorbia tirucalli 'Sticks on Fire'
furcraeas
Kalanchoe beharensis
Pachypodium lamerei
Portulacaria afra
yuccas

Midsize and Shrub Succulents

Midsize succulents—from 1 to 5 feet tall and wide—add verdure and interest to landscapes. Most make good fillers for garden beds, are short enough to go beneath windows, and work beautifully in one-plant containers. Repeat them for design continuity.

aeoniums
Agave americana 'Mediopicta Alba'
Agave angustifolia
Agave attenuata
Agave 'Baccarat'
Agave 'Blue Glow'
Agave bracteosa
Agave desmetiana
Agave multifilifera
Agave nickelsiae
Agave parryi
Agave potatorum
Agave 'Sharkskin'
Agave shawii
Agave victoriae-reginae
Agave vilmoriniana
Aloe arborescens
Aloe cameronii
Aloe camperi
Aloe dorotheae
Aloe maculata
Aloe ×nobilis
Aloe polyphylla
Aloe striata
Aloe vanbalenii
Aloe vera
Bulbine frutescens

cacti, spherical
Cistanthe grandiflora
Cotyledon orbiculata
Crassula capitella 'Campfire'
Crassula ovata
Crassula perfoliata var. *falcata*
Crassula sarcocaulis
dudleyas
Echeveria 'Afterglow'
Echeveria subrigida
Echinocactus grusonii
euphorbias, medusoid
Euphorbia milii
Euphorbia resinifera
Euphorbia trigona
Ferocactus species
Hesperaloe parviflora
kalanchoes
mangaves
Opuntia, dwarf varieties
Portulacaria afra 'Variegata'
sansevierias
sedums (shrub and most warm-
    climate varieties)
Senecio anteuphorbium
Senecio mandraliscae
Senecio vitalis

Small, Low-Growing, and Ground-Cover Succulents

Use diminutive succulents in containers and rock gardens, and to create rivers of color and texture in the landscape. Those that trail along the ground can also cascade over the sides of terraces, tall pots, and hanging baskets.

Aloe brevifolia
Aloe distans
Aloe, dwarf cultivars
Aloe humilis
Cotyledon tomentosa
Crassula multicava
crassulas, stacked
echeverias
×*Gasteraloe* 'Green Ice'
gasterias
Graptopetalum paraguayense
graptoverias
haworthias
hoyas

ice plants (*Delosperma, Drosanthemum, Lampranthus, Malephora*, mimicry plants)
Kalanchoe tomentosa
Lewisia species
Mammillaria species
Orostachys species
Othonna capensis
Portulacaria afra 'Minima'
sedums
sempervivums
Senecio radicans
Senecio rowleyanus

Succulents Variegated with Cream, White, or Yellow

Aeonium 'Kiwi'
Aeonium 'Sunburst'
Agave americana 'Marginata'
Agave americana 'Mediopicta Alba'
Agave angustifolia 'Marginata'
Agave attenuata 'Variegata'
Agave desmetiana 'Variegata'
Agave lophantha 'Quadricolor'
Agave nickelsiae
Agave victoriae-reginae
Agave vilmoriniana 'Stained Glass'
Agave weberi 'Arizona Star'
Aloe maculata
Aloe ×*nobilis* 'Variegata'

Crassula ovata 'Tricolor'
Euphorbia ammak 'Variegata'
Furcraea foetida 'Mediopicta'
×*Gasteraloe* 'Green Ice'
Kalanchoe fedtschenkoi 'Variegata'
Portulacaria afra 'Variegata'
sansevierias
Sedum spurium 'Tricolor'

Succulents with Warm-Hued Leaves

In addition to every shade of green, succulents come in yellow, orange, red, crimson, and purple, plus glowing pastels and shades of gray. Brilliant leaves tend to revert to green in too little light (the more sun, the more color). Use rosette succulents to create the look of a flower bed that's always in bloom and to repeat and contrast colors of adjacent design elements, such as walls, pots, outdoor furniture, and garden art.

Yellow
Aeonium 'Sunburst'
Crassula ovata 'Hummel's Sunset'
Disocactus species
Echinocactus grusonii
Sedum adolphi
Sedum 'Lime Twister'
Sedum makinoi 'Ogon'
Sedum rupestre 'Angelina'

Warm reds, orange, and rust
Aeonium 'Jack Catlin'
Aloe cameronii
Aloe dorotheae
Aloe, dwarf cultivars
Aloe ×*nobilis*
Aloe vanbalenii
Crassula capitella 'Campfire'
Crassula corymbulosa 'Red Pagoda'
Crassula pubescens
Echeveria agavoides 'Lipstick'
Euphorbia tirucalli 'Sticks on Fire'
Ferocactus latispinus
graptosedums
Kalanchoe luciae
Kalanchoe orgyalis
Sedum nussbaumerianum
Sedum ×*rubrotinctum* 'Pork and
    Beans'

Rose, maroon, lavender, and purple
Aeonium 'Jack Catlin'
Aeonium 'Zwartkop'
Aloe brevifolia
Echeveria cultivars
graptopetalums
graptoverias
Kalanchoe fedtschenkoi
Opuntia santa-rita
sempervivums

Succulents with Blue, Blue-Gray, or Gray Leaves

Two or more succulents with blue or gray leaves can be used to create a surreal combination seldom seen in cultivated gardens. Also effective is to contrast such plants with those with darker or reddish leaves, such as *Aeonium* 'Zwartkop' or *Kalanchoe luciae*, and with succulents and perennials that bloom in crimson, gold, or orange-yellow.

Aeonium haworthii
Agave americana
Agave 'Baccarat'
Agave 'Blue Flame'
Agave 'Blue Glow'
Agave franzosinii
Agave nickelsiae
Agave ovatifolia
Agave parryi
Agave potatorum
Agave 'Sharkskin'
Aloe brevifolia
Aloe humilis
Crassula perfoliata var. *falcata*
Crassula perforata
Dasylirion wheeleri
dudleyas
Echeveria imbricata and cultivars
Euphorbia polygona 'Snowflake'
Graptopetalum paraguayense
Kalanchoe beharensis
Kalanchoe tomentosa
Orostachys species
Pilosocereus pachycladus
Sedum burrito
Sedum dasyphyllum
Sedum rupestre 'Blue Spruce'
sempervivums
Senecio mandraliscae
Senecio serpens
Yucca rostrata

Succulents with Dramatic Blooms

Many succulents produce vivid, long-lasting flowers. In spring, entire hillsides of temperate-climate gardens are blanketed with brilliant ice plants. Aloes send up candelabra-shaped spires which, depending on the variety, can be several feet tall and corn-cobbed with orange-red buds. Flowers of *Kalanchoe blossfeldiana* hybrids, commonly sold as tabletop plants, come in numerous hues and blends. Succulents that have flowers atop thin stems, such as poppylike purple cistanthes and airy orange and yellow bulbines, are beautiful when massed. Succulents that die after flowering, such as agaves, aeoniums, and furcraeas, are not included here because they're grown mainly for their foliage.

aloes (except dwarf varieties)
beaucarneas
Bulbine frutescens
cacti
Cistanthe grandiflora
Cotyledon orbiculata
Crassula perfoliata var. *falcata*
dasylirions
dudleyas
epiphyllums
Euphorbia milii
Kalanchoe blossfeldiana
Kalanchoe luciae
kalanchoes classified as
    bryophyllums
sedums (shrub varieties)
yuccas

Top Fifty
Waterwise
Companion Plants
for Succulents

Numerous ornamental landscape plants perform well in conditions similar to those in which succulents thrive. The trees, shrubs, ground covers, bulbs, annuals, and perennials presented here have practical merits as well as beauty. They're low water and low maintenance, and from a design standpoint repeat or contrast aspects of succulents without upstaging them—except perhaps when in bloom or by sheer size.

Keep your garden's style in mind as you evaluate potential succulent companions. Palms and cycads, for example, lend a tropical ambience. Trees for desert-inspired gardens tend to have slender leaves and an open structure, such as palo verde and shoestring acacia. Mediterranean gardens practically beg for pride of Madeira, fruitless olive trees, and lavender. Bougainvillea, orange poppies, bird of paradise, and geraniums (pelargoniums) say southern California.

One way to create an interesting, cohesive garden is by selecting companions that share a common origin. For example, combine acacias, grevilleas, and kangaroo paws from Australia; California natives such as monkey flower, erigeron, penstemon, salvia, and ceanothus; or any number of shrubs in the protea family from South Africa.

For a texture garden, incorporate low-water grasses such as orange sedge, blue fescue, and purple fountain grass. Or edibles: citrus, rosemary, lavender, and daylilies. Use vivid bromeliads to enhance a bright-shade or coastal succulent garden. And if your priorities are great foliage and floral color, many of these favorites offer those as well.

Unless otherwise noted in their descriptions, the plants listed in this chapter share these cultivation requirements with succulents:

- prefer soil that drains well and is moderately fertile but not necessarily richly amended

- are drought tolerant and need minimal water once established

- do best in full sun or dappled shade (bright shade in desert areas)

- don't grow well with excessive rainfall or high humidity

- can tolerate some frost but do best when temperatures stay above freezing

- thrive in areas with hot, dry summers when watered regularly

For greater detail on the growth habits and requirements of these and other dry-climate plants, consult the experts at your local nursery or a trusted garden guide. In areas with desert heat or prolonged cold at or below freezing, make sure the plants you choose are known to withstand such extremes. As you plan your landscape, pay particular attention to the sizes given for mature specimens. Position small ones so they won't be engulfed, and make sure large ones have room to grow.

FEATURED GARDEN

A naturalist's garden near Santa Cruz

Neighbors shook their heads when they heard Stephanie Mills intended to create a large garden at her ranch in northern California, high atop a hill facing the Pacific. Formerly used for agriculture, Laguna Ranch's 372 acres had degraded into thistles, poison oak, and burr clover. Much of the soil is chalky mudstone that drains poorly in winter and dries out in summer. Also to contend with are rattlesnakes, wild boars, and coyotes. "And bobcats," Mills says, "but they do help with the gophers."

An avid naturalist raised in England, Mills inherited a passion for gardening from her mother and aunts. "I can lay out a hundred plants in twenty minutes," she says. "And I'm not afraid to experiment." The result is a colorful, textural blend of ornamental grasses, cordylines, proteas, and succulents growing in well-draining, amended soil in elevated areas and in terraced rock walls. Begun in 1991, the garden (which includes a dozen theme areas) has been hailed by *Pacific Horticulture* magazine as "world class."

Irrigation, a combination of drip and overhead, "is long and infrequent," Mills says. She describes the ranch's microclimate as "moderate, with summer fog and infrequent frost, and a few days of very hot temps." Because "wind accelerates as it comes up the slope from the ocean," the land has good airflow. Mills considers herself the curator of a plant collection that now numbers in the thousands of species. A room in her home showcases garden treasures: skulls of small rodents, snake skins, birds' nests, and exquisite sketches by visiting artists. Thanks to her "deep commitment to the garden archive," it also includes the images shown here.

Dusty miller (*Jacobaea maritima*) repeats the silvery blue of the potted agave while providing texture and color contrast to aloes and *Cordyline australis* (at upper left). Pincushion proteas (*Leucospermum cordifolium*) are the same orange as aloe flowers, foreground.

Enhancing a pathway in Stephanie Mills's garden are *Leucadendron* 'Wilson's Wonder' (at right) and white *Libertia grandiflora* (a bulb). The ice plant at center repeats the orange of aloes in bloom. Adding sword-shaped leaves are a variegated yucca and phormium and, at upper right, burgundy *Cordyline australis*.

Forming overlapping layers of color and texture in the Mills garden are a silver puya at right; *Agave stricta*, green aeoniums, a red cordyline, and *Dasylirion wheeleri* (foreground); *Agave* 'Blue Glow' and red and cream leucadendrons; large gray-green rosemary shrubs; and in the background a golden cypress.

'Mahogany' echeverias repeat the red of the leucadendron, and the shrub's coral is echoed by leucospermum flowers at upper left. Dasylirions provide upright interest and contrast texturally with a blue variety of *Agave attenuata*.

Stachys byzantina (lamb's ears) repeats the color of dudleya leaves while contrasting with the succulents' forms.

Shoestring acacias (*Acacia stenophylla*) arch over large variegated furcraeas. *Aloe plicatilis* fills the foreground.

Amaryllis belladonna blooms in a Portland, Oregon, garden that includes a hardy opuntia, dasylirions, and yuccas.

Acacia

evergreen or deciduous shrubs or trees
size varies; average 15 feet tall

The dozen or more species of *Acacia* sold in nurseries produce masses of fluffy, ball-shaped yellow flowers in midwinter and range from low-growing shrubs to tall, spreading trees. Good choices for succulent gardens include *A. cultriformis* (knife leaf acacia), a multistemmed shrub with short, pointed, silvery gray leaves; *A. baileyana*, with fine, ferny, gray-green foliage (cultivar 'Purpurea' has purple new growth); *A. longifolia*, with long, tapered inch-wide green leaves; and *A. stenophylla* (shoestring acacia) with stringy leaves and mahogany-colored bark. Plants tend to be short lived (fifteen to twenty years) and shallow rooted. Overwatering can cause rapid growth that weakens the tree. Don't plant in exposed areas prone to gusty winds, or near areas (such as pools) where leaf debris could be a problem.

Amaryllis belladonna

belladonna lily, naked ladies

bulb
leaves 18 inches tall; flower stalks 2 to 3 feet; bulbs spread to 2 feet or more

Onion-size bulbs store water during winter rains and need little or no irrigation thereafter. Lush, strap-shaped foliage is present through winter and spring and then dies back. In late summer, sweetly scented, pink lily-like flowers appear on leafless stems that rise from the exposed tops of bulbs—hence the common name naked ladies. Bulbs are long lived, like to be crowded, and may not bloom for a year or more if disturbed.

Yellow and red K-paws rise above the magenta, poppylike flowers of succulent *Cistanthe grandiflora.*

Anigozanthos flavidus

kangaroo paw, K-paw

evergreen perennial
foliage 2 to 3 feet tall; stems to 5 feet

The tubular, furry flowers of kangaroo paw come in shades of yellow, red, and green. Blooms line branching stalks; foliage is slender and upright. Flowers attract hummingbirds and are good in cut arrangements. Plant in well-drained, sandy soil, and repeat for best effect. Will bloom continuously from late spring into autumn if deadheaded. Good for lending color, texture, and vertical interest to in-ground succulent gardens. Use dwarf varieties in containers.

Bismarckia nobilis

Bismarck palm

evergreen tree
40 to 50 feet tall, 20 feet wide

Broad fronds and a statuesque silhouette make Bismarck palms highly desirable statement plants. The trees, from Madagascar (as are many succulents), provide a microclimate for plants growing beneath them and echo the silvery gray of cotyledons, agaves, and more. Over time, a Bismarck palm will get enormous; fronds can attain 10 feet in width. Both silver and green varieties exist; the former is more frost tolerant (to 25°F).

Bougainvillea

evergreen vining shrubs
15 to 30 feet

Bougainvillea's papery bracts come in brilliant colors—red, purple, orange, pink, golden yellow, and white—and its spreading, mounding growth habit enhances walls, archways, pergolas, slopes, terraces, and fences. Cultivars with variegated leaves are available. Bougainvillea makes a dynamic backdrop for large-leaved succulents such as agaves. The plants thrive in heat and full sun but aren't frost hardy.

Brahea armata, upper left, repeats the blue-gray of agaves in Kelly Griffin's garden. At upper right is *Bismarckia nobilis*. Catching the sun and repeating elements of other plants (fronds and a fountain shape) is a young cycad—*Encephalartos longifolius*.

Glossy leaved bronze, red, and burgundy bromeliads repeat the orange of dwarf aloes and coppertone stonecrop and contrast with a blue senecio and green echeverias.

Brahea armata

Mexican blue fan palm

evergreen tree
to 20 feet tall

This low-water palm handles heat, poor soil, and temperatures well below freezing. Many succulents are the same pale blue-gray, which creates pleasing repetitions in the garden. Mexican blue fan palms are slow growing, but even immature ones are worth having for their ornamental value.

Bromeliads

perennials
size varies

The majority of bromeliads are from humid jungles in Central and South America, and many come in vivid colors. If your garden is in a mild maritime location, use them to repeat the shapes of agaves and aloes and contribute bold sunset hues. The key to keeping tropical bromeliads looking good is to mist them daily, so have a spray bottle handy. Whereas succulents store water within their leaves, many bromeliads store it outside, in the cuplike center of the plant's rosette.

Callistemon viminalis 'Little John', in bloom at lower left, serves as a pathway border. Purple flowers at right are 'Martha Washington' pelargoniums. Canary Island date palms (top center and right) get by on rainfall alone, but before planting one, know that roots can break pipes and foundations; fronds require pruning and are sharp; and fruit can be messy.

Callistemon

bottlebrush

> evergreen shrubs or trees
> size varies from 3-foot dwarfs to 30-foot trees

Upward-arching bottlebrush shrubs and trees produce tufted flowers that resemble cylindrical brushes. The common tree variety, *Callistemon citrinus*, grows rapidly to 20 or 30 feet tall, needs little or no pruning, and makes a good hedge dotted with red. *Callistemon viminalis* (weeping bottlebrush) has pendant branches. An excellent dwarf variety, best planted in multiples, is *C. viminalis* 'Little John' (to 3 feet tall, sometimes called *C. citrinus* 'Little John'). Flowers attract hummingbirds.

Portulacaria afra 'Aurea' (foreground) and drifts of dainty sundrops echo the yellow leaf margins of *Agave vilmoriniana* 'Stained Glass'. At top right is *Cordyline australis* 'Torbay Dazzler'; at lower left, *Dymondia margaretae*, a tough nonsucculent ground cover.

Calylophus

sundrops

perennials
to 1 foot tall by several feet wide

Planted in drifts in the garden, yellow, poppylike sundrops suggest patches of sun shining through dappled leaves. These tough, hardy North America natives can handle temps below 0°F. Use them to repeat the yellow in succulents and other plants with variegated leaves. *Calylophus hartwegii* subsp. *lavandulifolius* is best for hot, dry gardens; *C. berlandieri* (also sold as *C. drummondianus*), for milder climates. Cut back in winter to tidy the plants and encourage lush spring growth.

Purple-blue *Ceanothus* 'Dark Star' is the color complement of yellow pincushion protea (*Leucospermum cordifolium*) and 'Gollum' jade. *Dasylirion longissimum* at lower left adds texture. Cotyledons in the pot and alongside it echo its celadon glaze.

Carex testacea

orange sedge

> ornamental grass
> 2 feet tall by 3 feet wide

This New Zealand grass has unusual bronze-colored, arching blades. Grow as a textural accent that contrasts with blue senecios and repeats the orange of stressed aloes, crassulas, and sedums. Make sure roots stay moist during hot, dry summers. Cold hardy to −10°F. Needs full sun and cool temps for best color.

Ceanothus

California lilac

> evergreen shrubs or ground covers
> size varies depending on species

Entire hillsides in chaparral areas of California turn blue in late February and early March when the "wild lilac" blooms. Fragrant flower clusters in pale blue, indigo, purple, or white are good for providing layers of color amid backdrop shrubs. Does best when grown with other natives. Plants tend to be short lived in cultivation; choose named varieties for best results.

Thriving beneath the cloudlike canopy of *Cercidium* 'Desert Museum' are 'Blue Glow' agaves, hesperaloes, dasylirions, *Opuntia* 'Santa Rita', purple fountain grass, and at lower right, *Penstemon heterophyllus* 'Margarita BOP' (blue bedder penstemon).

Cercidium

palo verde

> deciduous tree
> 25 to 30 feet tall

The common name palo verde means green stick in Spanish, which describes the tree's most distinctive characteristic: its green limbs. *Cercidium* is native to the Southwest and adjacent areas of Mexico. Trees form a broad, airy crown massed with dainty yellow flowers in spring and summer. To encourage deep roots, water young palo verde trees thoroughly but infrequently (twice a month in dry seasons) until established, at which point they need no irrigation; frequent light watering can lead to shallow roots, rapid growth, limbs that break easily, and toppling in windstorms. The hybrid *Cercidium* 'Desert Museum' flowers profusely, is thornless, and produces less leaf litter than the species.

Due to its tolerance for cold winds, salt spray, and sandy soil, *Cistus purpureus* is a good choice for seashore gardens. At left is *Echium fastuosum* (pride of Madeira).

Cistus

rockrose

> evergreen shrubs
> size depends on variety

The several species and numerous cultivars of rockrose are easy-care evergreen shrubs massed with round, crinkly, single-petaled white or pink flowers from spring into early summer (sporadic bloom thereafter). Soft-looking gray-green foliage makes a pleasant, low-maintenance backdrop for succulents large and small. Good in rock and boulder gardens and as erosion-control for steep slopes, plants handle frost and desert heat but lose fluffiness over time; replace when old and woody.

Citrus

orange, lemon, lime, grapefruit, and so on

> evergreen trees and shrubs
> size depends on variety

Although at first glance citrus trees appear nothing more than big green mounds, their ornamental benefits are significant if subtle. Lemons and grapefruit echo the yellow of variegated agaves, daylilies, sundrops, and more. In midwinter, orange fruit repeats the color of aloe blooms, and in spring, California poppies. Mature citrus can survive months without water, but regular irrigation enhances crop production, as do seasonal applications of high-nitrogen fertilizer.

Cordyline 'Electric Pink' lends star quality to a combination of *Euphorbia characias* (chartreuse bracts at left), a red-and-green-leaved zonal geranium, and bright orange parrot's beak (*Lotus berthelotii*).

Cycads in Jeff Chemnick's garden in Santa Barbara, California, include, right to left, *Encephalartos* 'Cleopatra' (Chemnick's own hybrid); similarly blue *E. lehmannii*; and greener, more upright *Dioon purpusii*. The tree succulent at left is *Aloe* 'Hercules'.

Cordyline

evergreen shrubs or trees
size varies by species

Small cordylines lend interest to container gardens; large ones stand out in the landscape. Flexible, sword-shaped leaves that radiate from a central point create a silhouette similar to yuccas, to which cordylines are distantly related. Plants resemble phormiums but have trunks. Colors range from dark green through shades of bronze, maroon, and pink, plus combinations thereof. Most are hardy to the mid-20s F, with *Cordyline australis* easily surviving temperatures into the teens.

Cycads

evergreen palmlike shrubs
size varies

The several different genera of cycads, often confused with palms and ferns, are cone-bearing plants from the dinosaur era. Leaves that radiate upward from a trunklike stem create a silhouette similar to that of aloes and agaves. Foliage ranges through shades of gray, green, and blue; textures, from soft and spineless to stiff and prickly. The best-known cycad is the sago palm, which is not a palm but *Cycas revoluta*. Due to their exceptional forms, textures, and colors, *Encephalartos* species—especially those from South Africa—are highly sought after. Although from subtropical and tropical regions, many cycads tolerate a broad range of temperatures, including mild frosts. Species of *Encephalartos* and *Dioon*, for example, are cultivated throughout southern and central California, Arizona, Texas, and the southeastern United States.

Echium candicans, agaves, and yellow Euryops pectinatus blend on a steep slope in Del Mar, California.

Dymondia margaretae

evergreen ground cover
2 to 3 inches high; spreads indefinitely

This native of South Africa makes a good lawn substitute and low-water ground cover for high-traffic areas. You can even park cars on it. Plants with fleshy roots form an interlocking mat of slender green leaves with white undersides. Yellow flowers are insignificant and daisylike. I plant patches of dymondia amid succulents to enable access to the juicy leaved plants without crushing them underfoot.

Echium candicans

pride of Madeira

shrubby perennial
5 to 6 feet tall; 6 to 10 feet wide

Magnificent conical flower spikes in shades of blue and lavender rise several feet above pride of Madeira's gray-green leaves in spring. Use *Echium candicans* (formerly *E. fastuosum*) as a same-size companion for large aloes and agaves, or prune into a small tree to provide dappled shade for small succulents. (Wear gloves; little hairs on foliage can irritate skin.) Plants are short lived (five or six years) but replace themselves by reseeding.

On a slope in my garden in early spring, California poppies repeat the orange of a tangelo tree's fruit and nearly engulf an *Agave americana* 'Marginata'.

Erigeron karvinskianus

Santa Barbara daisy, Mexican daisy

perennial ground cover
10 to 20 inches high, several feet wide

Mounding shrubs with fine, wiry stems are massed with delicate, dime-size, daisylike flowers in pink or white. Plants provide textural contrast to succulents and are useful as gap fillers. Solo shrubs, because of their white flowers, stand out, so repeat elsewhere in the garden for continuity. Can be invasive if given rich soil and ample water. Cut back when rangy. Performs best in full sun if temperatures stay below 80°F. Cold hardy to 15°F.

Eschscholzia californica

California poppy

annual
plants to 12 inches; flowers 4 inches in diameter

This poppy relative and state flower of California announces spring by blanketing hillsides with bright orange blooms. Satiny, five-petaled flowers fold at night and on cloudy days. Feathery leaves repeat the gray-green of many succulents while offering pleasing textural contrast. California poppies are easy to cultivate by seed and once naturalized return year after year.

Gazanias (foreground) repeat the yellow of *Euonymus japonicus* 'Aureomarginatus' (golden euonymus, upper right) in my garden. Lavender-pink *Drosanthemum floribundum* flowers provide a color complement.

Euonymus japonicus

evergreen euonymus

> evergreen shrub
> size varies

Grown solely for their foliage (flowers are insignificant), named cultivars of *Euonymus japonicus* provide leaves variegated with bright yellow and cream on shrubs that range from 18 inches to 6 feet high. Can be trimmed to show the plant's branching structure or sheared to keep dense and compact. Plants thrive in a wide range of climates and soils. Give full sun and good air circulation to keep mildew and pests at bay.

Euphorbia characias

> shrubby evergreen perennial
> size varies

Shrub euphorbias grow so effortlessly in succulent gardens, they may be the perfect companion plants. Some have a tendency to reseed but seldom obnoxiously so. Varieties range from 2-foot-tall bushes with upright stems to blousy 4-foot shrubs with large domed flower heads (actually, multiple bracts surrounding tiny blooms). Colors range from golden chartreuse to blue-green variegated with white. After late-winter bloom, cut spent stalks to the ground.

Coppery leaves of *Euphorbia cotinifolia* stand out against a backdrop of sunlit pines. Upright, arching leaves of bird of paradise (*Strelitzia reginae*) at center mirror those of *Aloe striata*, foreground.

Euphorbia cotinifolia

copper tree, Caribbean copper plant

evergreen shrub or tree
10 to 15 feet tall; 6 to 12 feet wide

Oval leaves range in hue from red-orange to purple on this airy tree, which can be pruned to stay shrub size. Use it as a backdrop for blue-gray or orange succulents, such as agaves and blooming aloes. New plants can be started from cuttings (trimmed branches). *Euphorbia cotinifolia* is sensitive to strong sun and frost, and may suffer dieback when temperatures drop into the mid-40s F. Cold makes it lose its leaves, but if the tree is otherwise healthy, they will regrow when the weather warms. This Central America native does best in a mild coastal climate. Position it near a wall that absorbs heat during the late afternoon and radiates it at night.

Euryops pectinatus

shrubby evergreen perennial
3 to 6 feet tall and wide

Euryops pectinatus serves as an inexpensive, hassle-free filler shrub. Lacy foliage contrasts with hefty succulents and ceroids (columnar cacti). Yellow daisylike flowers bloom nearly nonstop and resemble those of yellow ice plants and *Othonna capensis*. Thrives in coastal gardens, grows in poor soils, tolerates desert heat, and is cold hardy to 20°F. Plants get rangy over time; cut back in winter.

Festuca glauca with Agave parryi var. truncata

Festuca glauca

blue fescue

> ornamental grass
> 12 inches high; 10 inches wide

This frost-hardy ornamental grass forms dense, slowly spreading tufts of threadlike leaves. Use it to echo the shape and color of blue agaves while lending contrasting texture. Blue fescue is also striking in contrast with orange- or red-leaved succulents, such as paddle plants (*Kalanchoe luciae*) and coppertone stonecrop (*Sedum nussbaumerianum*).

Gazania hybrids

African daisies

> perennial ground covers
> plants 6 inches high; flower stems 6 to 10 inches

Although some gardeners consider them weedy, gazanias are welcome to reseed in my garden wherever they wish. These South Africa natives produce brilliant daisylike blooms in cream, orange, scarlet, reddish brown, and combinations thereof. The first flush is in early spring, followed by a smattering through autumn. Undersides of deeply lobed leaves are silvery and sometimes hairy. Petals may have a dark starburst or ring of black dots surrounding the yellow center. Flowers close in low light.

A red-flowering grevillea in the foreground creates a colorful, textural vignette when combined with a variegated *Phormium tenax* (center), purple statice, red and yellow K-paws, and green aeoniums (far right).

Grevillea

evergreen shrubs or trees
6 to 12 feet tall

Numerous *Grevillea* cultivars form soft-looking, airy shrubs. Waxy flowers look like a cross between bottlebrush (*Callistemon*) and pincushions (*Leucospermum*), to which grevilleas are related. Like other plants native to Australia, grevilleas need coarse, fast-draining soil free of salt buildup. Plant failure can happen soon after applying fertilizer containing phosphorus, so read the label carefully—or simply don't fertilize. (This is also true of many leucadendrons and leucospermums.)

Helichrysum petiolare along the home's foundation serves as a backdrop for *Aloe marlothii* in bloom. Similar to the helichrysum's shape and growth habit is purple *Lantana montevidensis* in the foreground.

Daylilies look best planted in multiples.

Helichrysum petiolare

licorice plant

> perennial
> 3 feet tall, trailing stems to 4 feet

Silvery gray, pillowlike *Helichrysum petiolare* shrubs send forth lateral stems that intertwine pleasantly with neighboring plants. Use with large aloes to frame their sculptural shapes and contrast with their vivid-hued blooms. Helichrysum also makes a good border plant for walkways and is pretty tumbling over terraces. In some regions—particularly coastal northern California—spent blooms should be deadheaded before the plants reseed invasively. Variegated and chartreuse cultivars are available.

Hemerocallis hybrids

daylilies

> deciduous or evergreen perennials
> size varies according to variety

Few flowering perennials are as accommodating as daylilies. Reblooming plants produce flowers from spring through autumn, tolerate almost any kind of soil, and handle being over- or underwatered. Daylily hybrids come in a multitude of flower colors in all warm hues—yellow, orange, burgundy, pink, and red. Divide in fall.

Purple repeats in lantana (foreground), statice (*Limonium perezii*, center), and *Lavandula stoechas* (middle right). Santa Barbara daisy (*Erigeron karvinskianus*) contrasts texturally with white cacti while repeating their color. Yellow cones are aeonium blooms.

Lantana montevidensis

trailing lantana

> evergreen vining shrub
> 2 feet tall, with branches trailing several feet

Tiny flowers in thumb-size clusters come in solid colors and combinations ranging from red-orange-yellow to purple-yellow-pink. Leaves are small, glossy, and dark green. Plants get woody, so trim back hard before spring growth begins. This lantana makes an excellent bank cover and contrasts effectively with large succulents such as yuccas, agaves, aloes, and furcraeas. Tolerates desert heat but will die back if hit by frost (from which it usually recovers).

Lavandula

lavender

> evergreen shrubs
> size varies

Fragrant purple floral spires top slender stems; foliage is dense, ferny, and gray-green. Numerous varieties are quite cold hardy, and a few are suitable for desert gardens—among them *Lavandula angustifolia* (English lavender). Easy-care *L. stoechas* (French lavender) has boxlike blooms with rabbit-ear petals. For a colorful, textural vignette, plant lavender with *Euphorbia tirucalli* 'Sticks on Fire', *Agave americana* 'Marginata', and *E. ammak* 'Variegata'. Shear after flowering, twice a year, to keep shrubs tidy and encourage new growth.

Lavatera maritima

tree mallow

> evergreen shrub
> 6 to 8 feet tall; 4 feet wide

Lavatera maritima (formerly *L*. bicolor) has an open, airy branching structure and flowers that resemble single hollyhocks. Petals are satiny purple-pink and heart shaped, with a deeper magenta at the centers. Maple-shaped foliage repeats the gray-green of many succulents. Give full sun and prune back in autumn. Lovely when combined with statice or ice plants that bloom purple, pink, or yellow.

Leucadendron

cone bush

> evergreen shrubs or trees
> size varies

Tall, upright, slender stems of these members of the protea family are useful in fresh and dried floral arrangements, so not surprisingly the shrubs transform gardens into bouquets. Choose named hybrids for best performance and color. Widely grown 'Safari Sunset' has vivid red bracts, is cold hardy to 20°F, and tolerates poor soils. Avoid applying fertilizer containing phosphorus.

ABOVE *Buchloe dactyloides* 'UC Verde', a buffalo grass cultivar, stays green year-round in this Santa Barbara garden. It can be mowed several times a year or allowed to grow into a meadow 6 to 8 inches high.

OPPOSITE Tall stems and rosy orange bracts of sun-loving *Leucadendron* 'Safari Sunset' enhance a succulent garden that includes a blue senecio, red echeverias, and aeoniums. The ornamental grass *Carex testacea*, lower right, mirrors the leucadendron's color while providing contrasting texture.

Leucospermum

pincushion protea

> evergreen shrubs
> 4 to 12 feet tall, depending on variety

Pincushions are dazzling flowers—warm-hued, exotic, and long lasting (up to six months where winters are mild). The plants come from a summer-dry region of South Africa that has winter rainfall and nutrient-poor, acidic soil. Grow on a slope to enhance drainage, which must be superb. Although pincushions generally are intolerant of cold, a few cultivars—including *Leucospermum cordifolium* 'Flame Giant'—are winter hardy to 25°F once established. Avoid fertilizers containing phosphorus.

Limonium perezii

sea lavender, statice

> perennial
> to 3 feet tall with 2- to 3-foot flower clusters

Tiny, papery flowers that cluster atop stiff, branched stems work well in both fresh and dried floral arrangements. Large, leathery leaves at the base of flower stalks form dense clumps. Plants tolerate heat but not frost and prefer sandy, fast-draining soil. Statice blooms from late winter into spring, at the same time as many aloes; the two flower colors—purple and orange—complement each other. Naturalizes in frost-free coastal gardens.

Meadow grasses

> perennial grasses
> height varies

If you like the look of a meadow, plant a native grass that gets by on rainfall and leave it unmowed; depending on your region, options include fine fescue, buffalo grass, blue grama, and hair grass. If you like the look of a lawn, along the coast of southern California, *Buchloe dactyloides* 'UC Verde', a buffalo grass cultivar, needs mowing half as often as common fescue, is disease and pest resistant, and requires only 12 inches of water a year or less—a 75-percent savings over fescue and 30 to 40 percent less than bermuda, zoysia, and St. Augustine grasses.

A yellow-flowering mimulus, left, floats in a minimally watered garden alongside graptoverias and sedums in bloom, golden barrel cacti, agaves, and New Zealand flax (*Phormium* 'Maori Queen').

Mimulus

monkey flower

> shrubby perennials
> 3 or 4 feet tall, depending on variety

These fine-textured woody perennials are characterized by tubular, flared flowers that suggest grinning monkey faces. Blooms range in color from brown and orange through yellow, pink, and crimson. Most species are native to cool, frost-free areas of the Pacific coast. Grow in full sun near the ocean, part shade inland. Cut back to maintain compactness.

Myoporum parvifolium creates the look of a lawn in this streetside garden without needing mowing or much water. Large *Agave americana* (the species and 'Marginata') specimens stand out amid colorful bougainvilleas, reddish purple *Tradescantia pallida* 'Purpurea', and orange *Euphorbia tirucalli* 'Sticks on Fire'. A jacaranda tree at upper right balances the composition and enlivens it in late spring with lavender blooms.

Myoporum parvifolium

evergreen ground cover
3 to 6 inches high; spreads up to 9 feet

This trailing ground cover has dense green leaves the size of large grains of rice. Dime-size white flowers appear in summer. Myoporum fills in rapidly; space plants 6 to 8 feet apart. It's good on slopes and banks but won't handle foot traffic. Hybrids have red stems and purple-green new growth.

The olive tree at upper right lends height to a terrace in Rancho Santa Fe, California, planted with red pelargoniums, ceanothus, agaves, cistus, prostrate rosemary, a variegated furcraea, *Cycas revoluta*, *Cereus hildmannianus* 'Monstrosus', *Euphorbia milii*, and red bougainvillea.

Olea europaea

olive tree

> evergreen tree
> 30 feet tall

Olive trees have been cultivated for centuries for their fruit, silvery green foliage, and gnarled limbs. Well-irrigated young trees can grow 5 to 6 feet a year; mature ones need only rainfall. These trees repeat the color of many succulents, lend textural contrast, are interesting at eye level, and provide a canopy that protects tender succulents from winter frost and searing summer sun. Prune to show branching structure. Unless you really want olives, a fruitless variety is advisable.

In a seasonal planting at Cistus Nursery near Portland, Oregon, multicolored leaves of zonal geraniums (*Pelargonium* 'Contrast') repeat the colors and variegations of a 'Sunburst' aeonium and a striped phormium.

Pelargonium

geranium

> shrubby or vining perennials
> shrubs to several feet tall and wide; vining
> varieties to 5 feet in length

Plants in the genus *Pelargonium* (commonly called geranium but not to be confused with true *Geranium*, or cranesbill) bloom in shades of white, pink, purple, magenta, and red. Pastel varieties blend with the muted colors of many succulents; more vivid pelargoniums contrast well with blue-leaved succulents such as *Senecio mandraliscae*. Those described as zonal have leaves banded with chartreuse, burgundy, and/or cream. Like poppies, nasturtiums, and daisies, vining species (commonly called ivy geraniums) flirt effectively with large agaves, dasylirions, and sharp-leaved yuccas.

Pennisetum ×*advena* 'Rubrum'

purple fountain grass

> ornamental grass
> to 5 feet tall and wide

Burgundy leaves and feathery plumes make *Pennisetum* ×*advena* 'Rubrum' (formerly *P. setaceum* 'Rubrum') among the most desirable of ornamental grasses. Cut to the ground in winter to make way for fresh new growth. 'Rubrum' does not self-sow as much as *P. setaceum*, one of its parents. Blooms summer through autumn.

Penstemon

> perennials or evergreen shrubs
> to several feet tall, depending on variety

Native to the American West, penstemons provide airy dots of color on multistemmed shrubs. The narrow, tubular, bell-shaped blooms of these wildflowers are beloved by hummingbirds. A mere 10 percent of the 250 species are commonly found in nurseries; others can be tricky to grow in cultivated gardens due to an intolerance for rich soil and overwatering.

Russian sage in bloom creates a lavender-blue haze. It and *Romneya coulteri* (matilija poppy, with white flowers, at left) spread via underground runners, so give both lots of room. *Phlomis fruticosa* (Jerusalem sage) has yellow flowers on upright stems. At lower right is purple statice. Citrus trees provide a green backdrop.

Perovskia atriplicifolia

Russian sage

shrubby perennial
4 to 5 feet tall, 2 to 3 feet wide

Airy panicles of fuzzy, lavender-blue flowers align themselves along slender stems above loosely branched shrubs. Neither a sage nor from Russia, this tough Tibetan is resistant to heat and drought, tolerates nutrient-poor soil (if well drained), and can go well below zero. Plants bloom repeatedly spring through autumn if deadheaded and should be cut to the ground in winter. Lovely when contrasted with red-orange aloe spires.

Phlomis fruticosa

Jerusalem sage

shrubby perennial
4 feet tall and wide

This carefree multistemmed Mediterranean perennial has soft, feltlike leaves and buttered-popcorn flowers at intervals along tall, upright stems. Blooms spring and summer. Give full sun along the coast, afternoon shade inland. Frost hardy to 15°F. Sensitive to heat in excess of 90°F; water more in summer as temperatures rise. Repeat and contrast flower colors with yellow and purple ice plant and nonsucculent perennials such as daylilies, Russian sage, lavender, and statice.

Prostrate rosemary trails over a wall, its dainty flowers echoing the blue of a century plant behind it and senecio alongside it (at left). Enhancing the vignette are *Agave attenuata*, red bougainvillea, and (at right) the dark green fronds of *Cycas revoluta* (sago palm).

Phormium

New Zealand flax

evergreen perennials
size varies

With their upthrusting, sword-shaped leaves, phormiums make a striking backdrop either solo or en masse. Their spiky, fan-shaped silhouettes repeat those of yuccas, agaves, and cordylines. In summer, New Zealand flax produces tall, branching flower spikes that attract nectar-loving birds. Plants range from immense (to 8 feet tall and wide) to dwarf varieties perfect for containers. Olive-green and bronze varieties of *Phormium tenax* are most common, but do look for Maori hybrids that combine coral, cream, yellow, red, and/or burgundy.

Rosmarinus officinalis

rosemary

evergreen shrub
size varies

This widely grown, woody herb has finely textured dark green leaves that when new and tender can be used in cooking. Shrub rosemary grows 5 to 6 feet tall. When cascading over terraces and containers, prostrate varieties are dark green waterfalls that sparkle with tiny azure flowers. Repeat the sky-blue of the blooms with agaves and *Senecio mandraliscae*. Plants are tough, fragrant, and long blooming (autumn through spring). Prune regularly to keep compact.

At Kendrick Lake Park near Denver, *Salvia pachyphylla* (rose sage, at right) combines with *Yucca filamentosa* and blanket flower (*Gaillardia*).

Salvia

shrubby perennials
size varies

This largest genus of the mint family includes more than nine hundred species of multistemmed shrubs that produce bloom spires in nearly every hue. Salvias vary in their water needs, but many are quite drought tolerant. Because they have a propensity for mildew, grow where humidity is low and air circulation excellent. Prune in late winter or early spring when new growth emerges from the base. Good choices for succulent gardens include *Salvia aurea* (African sage), *S. greggii* (autumn sage), *S. leucantha* (Mexican bush sage), and *S. pachyphylla* (rose sage).

Strelitzia reginae

bird of paradise

evergreen perennial
5 to 6 feet high and wide

Leaves of these fan-shaped tropical shrubs are green-gray and oar shaped; flowers suggest exotic orange-and-blue birds. Plants bloom best during cooler months and when their tuberous roots are crowded. Give full sun to part shade (especially in desert climates) and protect from frost. Get young plants off to a good start with regular water and soil enriched with organic matter.

Decorative glass vessels give these birds of paradise something to squawk about.

In the San Diego Botanic Garden, *Tecoma stans* produces pendant bouquets of yellow flowers.

Tecoma stans

yellow bells

> evergreen shrub or tree
> to 25 feet (in frost-free areas)

Tecoma stans (formerly *Stenolobium stans*) provides floral color in autumn, when few other plants are in bloom. These large shrubs (or minitrees) are native to a large portion of the Americas, from Texas and Florida southward to Argentina. If tips of branches are nipped by frost, wait until weather warms before pruning—they'll protect the plant from additional damage. Makes a good screen or hedge that contrasts in form and texture with cacti and agaves, and that repeats the yellow of variegated succulents, daylilies, and ice plants.

Tradescantia pallida 'Purpurea'

> perennial
> 1 to 1½ feet; spreads indefinitely

With its reddish purple leaves, this creeping perennial from Mexico adds rich color to dry gardens and containers. Spreading clumps will grow through other plants, but not invasively so, and will visually knit them together. Leaves are long, tapered ovals; the pink flowers, small and insignificant. Unless the ground has frozen, don't remove tradescantia when frost melts its leaves; it'll bounce back in spring. Protect from intense sun and increase irrigation during hot, dry weather.

Metric Conversions and Plant Hardiness Zones

inches	centimeters	feet	meters
¼	0.6	¼	0.08
⅓	0.8	⅓	0.1
½	1.25	½	0.15
1	2.5	1	0.3
2	5.0	2	0.6
3	7.5	3	0.9
4	10	4	1.2
5	12.5	5	1.5
6	15	6	1.8
7	18	7	2.1
8	20	8	2.4
9	23	9	2.7
10	25	10	3.0

Temperatures

$°C = 5/9 × (°F–32)$

$°F = (9/5 × °C) + 32$

Plant hardiness zones

To see temperature equivalents and to learn in which zone you garden, see the U.S. Department of Agriculture Hardiness Zone Map at planthardiness.ars.usda.gov/PHZMWeb/

For Canada, go to planthardiness.gc.ca/

Public Gardens and Succulent Plant Sources

Botanic gardens and arboreta that include cacti and succulents in their collections offer opportunities to see mature and unusual specimens, often in landscape applications. Perhaps the best known is the Huntington Botanical Gardens in San Marino (a suburb of Los Angeles), but there are numerous others, particularly in southern California, coastal California from the Bay Area south, and Arizona (for desert-adapted succulents and cacti). Moreover, many nurseries, colleges, universities, and theme parks (such as the San Diego Zoo's Safari Park) have impressive collections and display gardens. Before visiting, call or check the locale's website for hours, which may vary seasonally.

For resources specific to your area, contact your local chapter of the Cactus and Succulent Society of America or CSSA (cssainc.org). The CSSA offers a wealth of information, and members are education oriented. In addition to hosting monthly meetings, larger CSSA chapters have annual or semiannual shows at which you can view and obtain collectible specimens, art pottery, and topdressings. Before visiting any grower, call ahead or peruse the business's website for hours of operation and to discern its specialty. If no street address is provided, chances are the owners require an appointment. Succulent and cactus nurseries also do a thriving business online.

Suggestions for Further Reading

Anderson, Edward F. 2001. *The Cactus Family*. Portland, OR: Timber Press.

Baldwin, Debra Lee. 2010. *Succulent Container Gardens*. Portland, OR: Timber Press.

———. 2013. *Succulents Simplified*. Portland, OR: Timber Press.

Bogh, Molly, and Bill Schnetz. 2014. *Life After Lawns*. CreateSpace.

Calhoun, Scott. 2011. *The Gardener's Guide to Cactus*. Portland, OR: Timber Press.

Chance, Leo J. 2012. *Cacti and Succulents for Cold Climates*. Portland, OR: Timber Press.

Court, Doreen. 2010. *Succulent Flora of Southern Africa*. Cape Town, South Africa: Stuick Nature.

Dortort, Fred. 2011. *The Timber Press Guide to Succulent Plants of the World*. Portland, OR: Timber Press.

Dunnett, Nigel, Dusty Gedge, John Little, and Edmund C. Snodgrass. 2011. *Small Green Roofs: Low-Tech Options for Greener Living*. Portland, OR: Timber Press.

Dunnett, Nigel, and Noël Kingsbury. 2004. *Planting Green Roofs and Living Walls*. Portland, OR: Timber Press.

Editors of Sunset Magazine. 2012. *The New Sunset Western Garden Book*. Birmingham, AL: Oxmoor House.

———. 2014. *Sunset Western Garden Book of Landscaping*. Birmingham, AL: Oxmoor House.

———. 2015. *Sunset Western Garden Book of Easy-Care Plantings*. Birmingham, AL: Oxmoor House.

Gilmer, Maureen. 2009. *Palm Springs–Style Gardening*. San Diego, CA: Sunbelt Publications.

Horvath, Brent. 2014. *The Plant Lover's Guide to Sedums*. Portland, OR: Timber Press.

Irish, Mary, and Gary Irish. 2000. *Agaves, Yuccas, and Related Plants: A Gardener's Guide*. Portland, OR: Timber Press.

Kapitany, Attila, and Rudolf Schulz. 2004. *Succulents: Propagation*. Teesdale, Australia: Shulz Publishing.

Kelaidis, Gwen Moore. 2008. *Hardy Succulents*. North Adams, MA: Storey Publishing.

Moore, Jeff. 2014. *Under the Spell of Succulents*. Malaysia: Tien Wah Press.

Penick, Pam. 2013. *Lawn Gone!* Berkeley, CA: Ten Speed Press.

———. 2016. *The Water-Saving Garden*. Berkeley, CA: Ten Speed Press.

Phillips, Judith. 2015. *Growing the Southwest Garden*. Portland, OR: Timber Press.

Pilbeam, John. 2008. *The Genus Echeveria*. Essex, England: British Cactus and Succulent Society.

Rubin, Greg, and Lucy Warren. 2016. *The Drought-Defying California Garden: 230 Native Plants for a Lush, Low-Water Landscape*. Portland, OR: Timber Press.

Silver, Johanna. 2016. *The Bold Dry Garden: Lessons from the Ruth Bancroft Garden*. Photos by Marion Brenner. Portland, OR: Timber Press.

Snodgrass, Edmund C., and Lucie L. Snodgrass. 2006. *Green Roof Plants: A Resource and Planting Guide*. Portland, OR: Timber Press.

Starr, Greg. 2012. *Agaves: Living Sculptures for Landscapes and Containers*. Portland, OR: Timber Press.

Sweet, Rebecca. 2013. *Refresh Your Garden Design with Color, Texture and Form*. Cincinnati, OH: Horticulture Books.

Walker, Don, and Steve Brigham. 2003. *Ornamental Trees of San Diego: Mediterranean Climate Trees for the Garden*. Encinitas, CA: San Diego Horticultural Society.

Acknowledgments

The more than 150 homeowners, nursery owners and managers, and floral and garden designers who made this book possible are listed in the design and location credits that follow. Individuals who were especially generous with their time and expertise include horticulturists Brian Kemble of the Ruth Bancroft Garden, Kelly Griffin of Altman Plants, and Wanda Mallen of the Palomar Cactus and Succulent Society. I am also grateful for the competent and friendly staff at Timber Press, the above-and-beyond guidance and expertise of editor Lorraine Anderson, and the limitless kindness and patience of my husband, Jeff Walz.

Photography, Design, and Location Credits

Photos are by Debra Lee Baldwin unless otherwise credited.

A   Ken and Deena Altman garden, Escondido, CA, 135, 144 top
Patrick Anderson garden, Fallbrook, CA, 14 top, 38 left, 61 both, 62, 171 right
Eric Arneson and Nahal Sohbati of the Academy of Art University for the
    San Francisco Flower & Garden Show, 66 left
Caitlin Atkinson Photography, 117
Wallace Austin bottle fish, 204 bottom left

B   Bacara Resort, Santa Barbara, CA, 60 left, 72
Peter Bailey garden, Escondido, CA, 50, 118 left
Alison Baldwin pottery, 11, 17 right, 38 middle
Art and Sandra Baldwin garden, San Diego, CA, 136 bottom, 216 right
Debra Lee Baldwin design, 10–11, 17–20, 38 middle, 48, 51 bottom
    right, 116 bottom left and right, 119 left, 122, 123 right, 134, 155, 157,
    202 bottom, 204 bottom left and bottom right, 210, 270
Debra Lee Baldwin garden, Escondido, CA, 10–11, 17–20, 39, 48, 119 top
    (both), 122, 123 right, 127, 134, 136 top, 157, 204 bottom left and bottom
    right, 210, 269, 270
Debra Lee Baldwin for Roger's Gardens Nursery, Corona del Mar, CA,
    192 top left
Debra Lee Baldwin for Weidners' Gardens nursery, Encinitas, CA, 218 left
Gary Bartl for the Battaglia residence, San Rafael, CA, 98 left
Adriana Basques Photography, 98 left
Bassage-Vinatieri garden, Santa Barbara, CA, 74, 174 bottom right,
    176 bottom left, 242, 244, 277
Jarrod Baumann of Zeterre Landscape Architecture, San Francisco, garden
    design and sculpture, 69 bottom
Jim Bishop garden, San Diego, CA, 31 top
Loree Bohl photo, 15
Megan Boone of Nature's Containers Vintage Garden Art for WaterWise
    Yard Design & Décor, Temecula, CA, 115 bottom
Brady Architectural Photography, 88–89, 116 top left and right

R   Mark Rafter pottery, 51 lower right
Dianne Reese of Well-Rooted Designs for Oasis Water Efficient Gardens
nursery, Escondido, CA, 115 top right
Beverly and Richard Reid garden, Christina Lake, BC, 113 top middle
John Robinson sculpture, 69 top
Mindy Rosenblatt and Evelyn Jacob garden, Santa Barbara, 36 top
Ruth Bancroft Garden, Walnut Creek, CA, 33, 147 top

S   San Diego Botanic Garden, Encinitas, CA, 207, 285 right
Santa Barbara Succulent Art for the Bacara Resort, Santa Barbara, CA, 60 left
Rob and Suzy Schaefer garden, Rancho Santa Fe, CA, 12, 63 right, 107 left,
166 right
Bill Schnetz of Schnetz Landscape for Inge Brown, Rancho Santa Fe, CA,
58 left
Seaside Gardens nursery, Carpinteria, CA, 43 left
Tiffany Sheele garden, Marina CA, 239 right
Sherman Gardens, Corona del Mar, CA, 261 right
Kyle Short Photography, 7 middle, 36 top and bottom, 46, 63 left, 65 both, 66
left, 67, 72, 82 top, 99 top, 100 top, 118 right, 138 left, 174 lower right, 177,
179, 220 right, 236 left, 237 top, 242, 245, 263, 267 right, 277, author photo
SJA Inc., Russ Johnston and Denny Smithgall for Soleil, San Diego, CA,
119 bottom
Joe Stead of Orange Coast College for Anton Segerstrom, Corona del Mar,
CA, 90
Succulent Café, Oceanside, CA, 9 right, 237 lower left and right
Succulent Gardens Nursery, Castroville, CA, 40, 100 bottom, 172, 189 top
right, 248
Chris and Margaret Sullivan garden, San Diego, CA, 104 both
Steve Sutherland of SSA Landscape Architects, Santa Cruz, CA, for the
Succulent Extravaganza at Succulent Gardens nursery, Castroville, CA,
100 bottom
Rebecca Sweet of Harmony in the Garden, Los Altos, CA for Kathy and
Steven Coutre, Stanford, CA; photo by Rebecca Sweet, 56 top

T   Margot S. Taylor, RLA, Landscape Architect, Land Ethics, LLC, Kennett
Square, PA, 110 top
Bill Teague for Janice Byrne, Del Mar, CA, 183 bottom
Bernard Trainor + Associates, Monterey, CA, 99 bottom
Mark Turner and Natalie McClendon garden, Bellingham, WA, 228 right
Mark Turner, Turner Photographics, 60 right, 77, 103, 105 top left, 113 top
middle and right

U   University of California, Davis collection, 200 top right

V   Alice van de Water garden, Santa Barbara, CA, 160
Jennifer Voss, Gardefacts Landscape Design, for Christine Anderson, Santa
Barbara, CA, 36 bottom, 55, 279
Jennifer Voss, Gardefacts Landscape Design, for Nancy Gunzberg, Santa
Barbara, CA 220 right

Index

KYLE SHORT

Popularly known as the Queen of Succulents, Debra Lee Baldwin specializes in showing how to use sculptural, water-wise, and easy-care succulents in a wide variety of creative and appealing applications. Debra, an award-winning garden photojournalist and author, launched the gardening world's interest in succulents with the first edition of *Designing with Succulents* in 2007. She went on to write two more Timber Press best sellers, *Succulent Container Gardens* and *Succulents Simplified*. A decade spent scouting and writing for top home and garden publications gave Debra the sophisticated, practical, and reader-friendly approach to design found in her books, newsletters, videos, live presentations, and classes. Debra's own half-acre garden near San Diego has been featured in *Better Homes & Gardens*, *San Diego Home/Garden* magazine, *Sunset*, and other publications. Visit her website at debraleebaldwin.com.